3

ECONOMIC ISSUES, PROBLEMS AND PERSPECTIVES

HIGH UNEMPLOYMENT

SELECT ANALYSES

ECONOMIC ISSUES, PROBLEMS AND PERSPECTIVES

Additional books in this series can be found on Nova's website under the Series tab.

Additional E-books in this series can be found on Nova's website under the E-book tab.

AMERICAN POLITICAL, ECONOMIC, AND SECURITY ISSUES

Additional books in this series can be found on Nova's website under the Series tab.

Additional E-books in this series can be found on Nova's website under the E-book tab.

ECONOMIC ISSUES, PROBLEMS AND PERSPECTIVES

HIGH UNEMPLOYMENT

SELECT ANALYSES

LESLIE SANDIDGE
AND
VICTOR IRBY
EDITORS

New York

For permission to use material from this book please contact us:
Telephone 631-231-7269; Fax 631-231-8175
Web Site: http://www.novapublishers.com

LIBRARY OF CONGRESS CATALOGING-IN-PUBLICATION DATA

ISBN: 978-1-62257-994-5

Published by Nova Science Publishers, Inc. † New York

CONTENTS

PREFACE

The rate of unemployment in the United States has exceeded 8 percent since February 2009, making the past three years the longest stretch of high unemployment in this country since the Great Depression. Such persistently high unemployment has wide-ranging repercussions. It places financial, psychological, and even physical strains on people who are unable to find work and on their families as well; it places budgetary pressures on the federal government and on state and local governments, as tax revenues decline and expenditures increase; and it results in a long-term erosion of skills that will reduce the nation's productivity and people's income in the future. This book examines a broad array of policy approaches designed to reduce unemployment. Some of those policies would aim to boost the economy and demand for goods and services, reflecting the fact that the increase in unemployment in particular in general and long-term unemployment in particular is primarily attributable to weak demand for labor, which in turn, is the result of weak aggregate demand.

Chapter 1 – This Congressional Budget Office (CBO) study, which examines the state of the labor market and a broad array of policy approaches designed to reduce unemployment, was prepared at the request of the Ranking Member of the House Committee on Ways and Means. In keeping with CBO's mandate to provide objective, impartial analysis, this study makes no recommendations.

Chapter 2 – The recession of 2007 to 2009 was the most severe in the United States since the 1930s, resulting in a net loss of 7.5 million jobs. Workers who lose a job through no fault of their own (referred to as "displaced workers" in this chapter) may turn to financial assistance offered through the Unemployment Insurance (UI) program. Currently, through benefit extensions authorized by Congress, eligible displaced workers can receive UI benefits for up to 99 weeks in certain states. However, with the slow economic recovery, some may exhaust UI benefits without finding a new job. This raises questions about how Temporary Assistance for Needy Families (TANF), a program that provides cash assistance to low-income families with children, and other support programs are aiding those who have exhausted UI benefits.

GAO was asked to examine: (1) how many of the workers who lost jobs in the recession received and exhausted UI; (2) what are the economic circumstances of those who exhausted UI, and how many received support from TANF and other programs; and (3) the extent to which UI agencies refer those exhausting UI to other support programs. GAO analyzed data from the Current Population Survey's 2008 and 2010 Displaced Worker Supplements and the 2010 Annual Social and Economic Supplement and data from the Departments of Labor and Health and Human Services. GAO also surveyed 51 state UI agencies and conducted interviews with 16 state TANF agencies, selected to reflect a range of unemployment rate changes in recent years.

GAO is making no recommendations in this chapter.

Chapter 3 – A persistently high unemployment rate is of concern to Congress for a variety of reasons, including its negative consequences for the economic well-being of individuals and its impact on the federal budget (i.e., deficit growth due to lower revenue and higher expenditures). The unemployment rate was 9.5% when the economy emerged from the 11th postwar recession in June 2009. It climbed further to peak at 10.1% in October 2009. The rate then slowly declined before stalling at about 9.0% for most of 2011. Although the unemployment rate has resumed its decline, at slightly above 8.0% in early 2012, it remains at an historically high level.

The slow rebound of the labor market has prompted calls for new measures to stimulate economic growth to avoid a so-called double-dip recession, such as occurred during the early 1980s. The economy contracted in July 1981, 12 months into the recovery from the January-July 1980 recession. The unemployment rate had not fallen to its pre-recession level before the 1981-1982 recession began. Some observers have from time to time expressed concern that another shock (e.g., the slowdown of European economies) might push the nation back into recession.

After most postwar recessions, it took at least eight months for the unemployment rate to fall by one full percentage point. The slowest decline occurred following the 2001 recession's end, when the unemployment rate was a comparatively low 5.5%. About 3 1/2 years elapsed before the rate fell just one-half of one percentage point. In contrast, the recovery from the severe

1981-1982 recession began with the highest unemployment rate of the postwar period (10.8%). In that instance, it took only eight months for the rate to fall over one percentage point. Some hoped the unemployment rate would fall as quickly after the Great Recession, but the speed of improvement has been more typical of the so-called jobless recovery from the 2001 recession.

What appears to matter for a reduction in the unemployment rate is the size of the output gap, that is, the rate of actual economic growth compared with the rate of potential output growth. Potential output is a measure of the economy's capacity to produce goods and services when resources (e.g., labor) are fully utilized. The growth rate of potential output is a function of the growth rates of potential productivity and the labor supply when the economy is at full employment. If potential output growth is about 2.5% annually at full employment, then the growth rate in real gross domestic product (GDP) would have to be greater to yield a falling unemployment rate. How much greater will determine the speed of improvement in the unemployment rate, according to a rule of thumb known as Okun's law.

Some observers recently have suggested that the decline in the unemployment rate from 9.0% in September 2011 to 8.5% in December 2011 defied Okun's law because real GDP growth appears to have been too low to have produced such a large fall in unemployment. With the Congressional Budget Office (CBO) projecting that real GDP growth will stay below potential output growth for years to come, the unemployment rate may remain about where it is today (above 8.0%) through 2014, before falling to less than 6.0% by 2017.

In: High Unemployment: Select Analyses ISBN: 978-1-62257-994-5
Editors: L. Sandidge and V. Irby

Chapter 1

UNDERSTANDING AND RESPONDING TO PERSISTENTLY HIGH UNEMPLOYMENT*

Congressional Budget Office

PREFACE

This Congressional Budget Office (CBO) study, which examines the state of the labor market and a broad array of policy approaches designed to reduce unemployment, was prepared at the request of the Ranking Member of the House Committee on Ways and Means. In keeping with CBO's mandate to provide objective, impartial analysis, this study makes no recommendations.

Douglas W. Elmendorf
Director

SUMMARY

The rate of unemployment in the United States has exceeded 8 percent since February 2009, making the past three years the longest stretch of high unemployment in this country since the Great Depression. Moreover, the

* This is an edited, reformatted and augmented version of a Congressional Budget Office publication, Pub. No. 4287, dated February 2012.

Congressional Budget Office (CBO) projects that the unemployment rate will remain above 8 percent until 2014. The official unemployment rate excludes those individuals who would like to work but have not searched for a job in the past four weeks as well as those who are working part-time but would prefer full-time work; if those people were counted among the unemployed, the unemployment rate in January 2012 would have been about 15 percent. Compounding the problem of high unemployment, the share of unemployed people looking for work for more than six months—referred to as the long-term unemployed—topped 40 percent in December 2009 for the first time since 1948, when such data began to be collected; it has remained above that level ever since.

Such persistently high unemployment has wide-ranging repercussions: It places financial, psychological, and even physical strains on people who are unable to find work and on their families as well; it places budgetary pressures on the federal government and on state and local governments, as tax revenues decline and expenditures increase; and it results in a long-term erosion of skills that will reduce the nation's productivity and people's income in the future.

In this study, CBO examines a broad array of policy approaches designed to reduce unemployment. Some of those policies would aim to boost the economy and demand for goods and services, reflecting the fact that the increase in unemployment in general and long-term unemployment in particular is primarily attributable to weak demand for labor, which, in turn, is the result of weak aggregate demand. Policies to increase demand for workers could reduce unemployment substantially in 2012 and 2013, although those policies could be costly to the federal government and would vary greatly in their effectiveness per dollar of budgetary cost. Other policies that CBO examined, including worker training, changes to the unemployment insurance (UI) system, and helping the unemployed transition to new jobs, would probably not have a significant effect on the overall unemployment rate during the next two years, primarily because of their limited scope, but they could provide support to certain groups and have longer-run positive effects.

Unemployment and Its Consequences

Households with unemployed workers are adversely affected by joblessness in many ways. For workers who have been displaced through no fault of their own— specifically, who lost or left a job because their plant or company closed or moved, because there was insufficient work for them to do or because their position or shift was abolished—the drop in earnings associated with losing a job during a recession may persist for many years, even when these workers eventually find a new job. Older workers and those with long tenure in their previous job are especially vulnerable because new jobs for those workers typically pay less and offer less potential for earnings growth. Other types of unemployed workers—for example, people entering the labor market for the first time (typically after completing school)—are also adversely affected by a weak economy. People who start their career in times of high unemployment tend to have persistently lower earnings than their counterparts who begin seeking work under better economic circumstances.

In addition to its immediate and lasting effects on earnings and family finances, unemployment is also correlated with deteriorating mental and physical health and with increased mortality. A parent's job loss can lead to worse schooling outcomes for children and, ultimately, to worse labor market outcomes for those children once they become adults. In those and other ways, unemployment is costly for many households, and the adverse effects are probably worse for those unemployed for an extended period.

Factors Causing High Unemployment

Many factors are responsible for the rise in unemployment in general and in long-term unemployment in particular. Explanations include the following:

- Weak demand for goods and services, as a result of the recession and its aftermath, which results in weak demand for workers;
- Mismatches between would-be employers' needs and the skills or location of the unemployed;
- Incentives from extensions of unemployment insurance for people to stay in the labor force and continue searching for work; and
- The erosion of unemployed workers' skills and the belief held by some employers that people who have been unemployed for a long time would be low-quality workers (a phenomenon sometimes called stigma).

Slack demand for goods and services (that is, slack aggregate demand) is the primary reason for the persistently high levels of unemployment and long-term unemployment observed today, in CBO's judgment; other factors appear to play smaller roles. However, when aggregate demand ultimately picks up, as it eventually will, so-called structural factors—specifically, employer-employee mismatches, the erosion of skills, and stigma—may continue to keep unemployment and long-term unemployment higher than normal.

Policies to Increase Demand for Workers

In previous work, CBO examined the possible effects of a number of policies designed to increase output and employment in 2012 and 2013.[1] Those fiscal policy actions were intended to increase demand for goods and services and raise employment in three key ways: by boosting households' disposable income, by providing support to businesses, and by increasing aid to state governments or government spending on infrastructure. Initiatives that would reduce the marginal cost to businesses of adding employees or that would target people most likely to spend the additional income (generally, people with lower income) would have the largest effects on employment per dollar of budgetary cost in 2012 and 2013, CBO found. Policies primarily affecting businesses' cash flow would have little impact on their marginal incentives to hire or invest and, therefore, would have only small effects on employment per dollar of budgetary cost.

Despite the near-term economic benefits, such actions would add to the already large projected budget deficits that would exist under current policies, either immediately or over time. Unless other actions were taken to reverse the accumulation of government debt, the nation's output and people's income would ultimately be lower than they otherwise would have been. To boost the economy in the near term while seeking to achieve longterm fiscal sustainability, a combination of policies would be required: changes in taxes and spending that would increase the deficit now but reduce it later in the decade.

Lawmakers could also influence employment—and unemployment—during the next few years by changing policies that do not involve, or whose scope extends well beyond, taxation and government spending. In its previous work, CBO considered some potential changes in regulatory and other policies related to energy and the environment, the financial and health care sectors, and international trade. In CBO's judgment, the economic effects of the changes in regulatory policies or other types of policies that the agency examined—apart from fiscal policies—probably would be too small, or would occur too slowly, to significantly alter overall output or employment in the next two years.

Other Policies to Reduce Unemployment

Lawmakers could aim to reduce unemployment by addressing factors other than weak demand for goods and services. In this chapter, CBO examines initiatives that would take the following approaches:

- Improving workers' skills,
- Modifying the unemployment insurance program, or Facilitating transitions to work.

Examples include training programs (perhaps targeted at specific vocations, geographic areas, or age groups); changes to unemployment insurance to encourage unemployed people to return to work quickly, keep the unemployed connected to the workplace, or forestall job losses; and programs such as job-search assistance and housing-mobility assistance that help the unemployed transition to new jobs and locations. Such policies could be implemented using mechanisms ranging from providing funding through block grants to direct federal operation. But such policies would probably not have a significant effect on unemployment over the next two years, primarily because the policies the agency examined could probably not be implemented on a sufficiently large scale during that time. However, by reducing the extent of unemployment and long-term unemployment in the future, they might have longer-term benefits.

UNDERSTANDING AND RESPONDING TO PERSISTENTLY HIGH UNEMPLOYMENT

Unemployment and Its Consequences

The effects of the recent recession, which began in December 2007 and ended in June 2009, have combined to make the years since 2007 the worst period of unemployment in the United States since the 1930s. Contributing factors include the following:

- The unemployment rate reached a very high level, peaking at 10.0 percent in October 2009. That rate has been topped in the post–World War II period only once before—during the severe 1981–1982 recession (see the upper panel of Figure 1). From the end of 2007 to

October 2009, the number of unemployed people rose by almost 8 million. (For details about how unemployment is defined and measured, see Box 1.)

- Unemployment has been high for an extended period. As of January 2012, the unemployment rate had been above 8 percent for 36 months and at or above 9 percent for 28 of the preceding 36 months. In contrast, the unemployment rate exceeded 8 percent for 26 months and was at or above 9 percent for 19 months during the recession of the early 1980s.
- Many people would like to work but have not searched for a job in the past four weeks, or are working part-time but would prefer full-time work. If those people were counted among the unemployed, the unemployment rate in January 2012 would have been about 15 percent.
- The share of unemployment accounted for by the long-term unemployed (people who have been seeking work for more than 26 weeks) has been at an all-time high. Over 40 percent of people who are currently unemployed have been out of work for more than half a year, as compared with about one-quarter during the 1981–1982 recession (see the lower panel of Figure 1).[1]

The extent of long-term unemployment is much greater than would be expected on the basis of its historical relationship with the overall unemployment rate (see Figure 2 on page 4).

Had long-term unemployment followed its historical pattern, it would have been between 20 percent and 25 percent of total unemployment in 2009 and 2010, rather than over 40 percent. That high share means that many of the same people have been unemployed from month to month and from year to year.[2] As a result, much of the impact of unemployment has fallen on people who have been unemployed for a long time rather than being shared by a wider set of people unemployed for shorter periods.

Characteristics of the Unemployed

People are generally categorized as unemployed if they meet the following criteria:

- They have lost a job (usually as a result of a layoff) or have left their previous job voluntarily and are actively seeking work; or

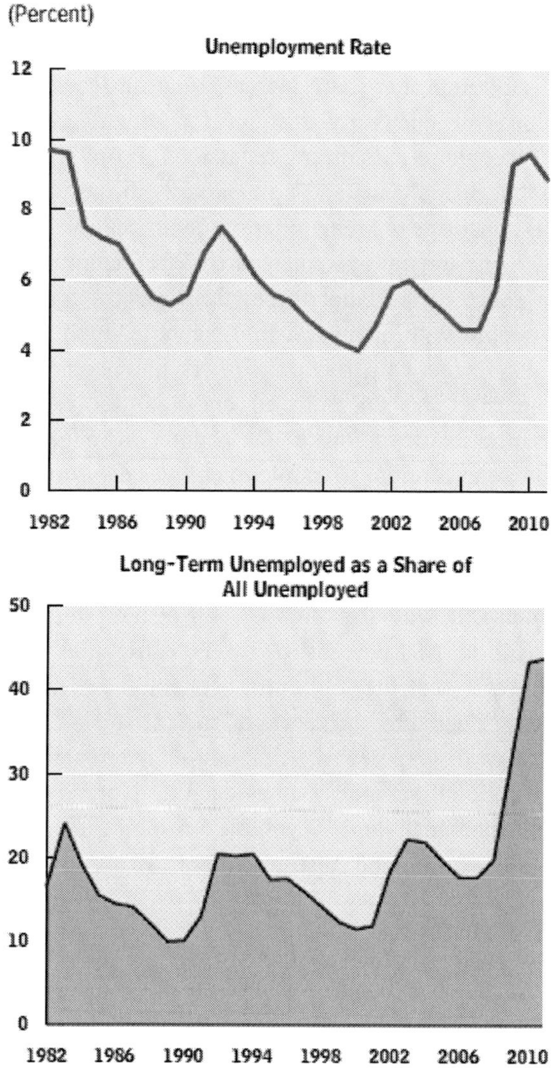

Source: Bureau of Labor Statistics.

Notes: The long-term unemployed have been unemployed for more than 26 weeks. Data are based on the portion of the population ages 16 andolder.

Figure 1. The Unemployment Rate and the Long-Term Unemployed as a Share of All Unemployed, 1982 to 2011.

- They have recently entered the labor force (for instance, after leaving school for the first time) or reentered the labor force and are seeking work.

People who have been laid off typically account for about 50 percent of the unemployed, although that share increases during recessions. People who quit their previous job generally account for roughly 10 percent of the unemployed, but that share falls during recessions. People reentering the labor force (usually about 30 percent) and new entrants to the labor force (usually about 10 percent) constitute the remainder of the unemployed.

People who were unemployed in March 2011 came disproportionately (relative to their share of the labor force) from certain demographic groups, including men, people with at most a high school diploma, married people, African Americans, former construction workers, and people under age 25 (see Table 1 on page 5). The unemployed and long-term unemployed were distributed across the major regions of the country in rough proportion to the labor force, with one exception: Unemployment was disproportionately high in the West. Broad regional categories mask significant variation among states, however. For instance, although the unemployment rate in December 2011 was particularly high in western states such as California (11 percent) and Nevada (13 percent), it was also high in nonwestern states hit hard by the mortgage crisis (Florida, 10 percent) or by the difficulties of the automobile industry (Michigan, 9 percent). In contrast, unemployment rates were much lower in states less affected by those events, such as Iowa (6 percent), Virginia (6 percent), and Hawaii (7 percent). Although their populations are too small to greatly affect regional statistics, states such as North Dakota (3 percent), South Dakota (4 percent), and Wyoming (6 percent) all had very low unemployment rates, in part because of a boom in the oil industry in those locales.

Box 1. Defining Unemployment

The Bureau of Labor Statistics (BLS) compiles labor force statistics and computes the unemployment rate using data from the Current Population Survey, a monthly survey of households that is conducted for BLS by the Census Bureau. On the basis of participants' responses to the survey, adult respondents are assigned to one of three labor force categories:

- Respondents are categorized as *employed* if they have a job or are self-employed at the time of the survey.

- They are categorized as *unemployed* if they do not have a job but would like one and are actively searching for a position. Respondents in both categories—employed and unemployed—are considered to be *in the labor force*.
- Respondents who are neither working nor looking for work are characterized as *out of the labor force*. People classified as out of the labor force include retirees, full-time students who do not have a job, and full-time, unpaid caregivers.

The *unemployment rate* is then calculated as the fraction of the labor force that is unemployed.

The distinction between people categorized as employed and those in the other two categories is relatively clear-cut. Ambiguities sometimes arise for people who are employed but work fewer hours per week than they would like or who are working at jobs that do not fully utilize their skills. Such workers are sometimes described as *underemployed*, but that designation is not recognized by BLS as a separate category. The distinction between being unemployed and out of the labor force is less clear-cut. Each group consists of people who are jobless, of course, but questions arise as to how to treat respondents who would like to work if a suitable job was available but who have stopped looking for work.

Because they are no longer looking for work, such respondents would *not* be considered unemployed and would instead be classified as out of the labor force. In some alternative categorizations, used by BLS and by other analysts, such respondents are characterized as *discouraged workers* and included with the unemployed as a measure of those who would like a job but currently do not have one.

Effects of Job Loss and Unemployment on Workers and Their Families

Unemployment, and especially long-term unemployment, often leads to adverse consequences for unemployed workers and their families. Various federal programs assist unemployed people by providing income and other support, including some programs that are targeted particularly at those with low family income or disabilities (see Box 2). Nevertheless, the effects of unemployment may be prolonged and may affect workers' subsequent earnings, their health, and their family's well-being.[3]

Reduced Earnings After Job Loss

For many displaced workers—those who permanently lose their job through no fault of their own—the effects on subsequent earnings can be substantial. They initially suffer a decline in earnings when they become unemployed. But displaced workers also often suffer longer-term losses in earnings from a combination of factors: reduced rates of employment, fewer hours worked, and lower hourly wages once they find a new job. Data compiled by the Bureau of Labor Statistics (BLS) show that, among workers meeting the following criteria—they lost a full-time job between 2007 and 2009, had three or more years of tenure when they lost that job, and were working again in January 2010— 55 percent earned less per week than they had at their previous job, and 36 percent took at least a 20 percent cut in weekly earnings.[4] Job loss is not always a financially costly event, as 45 percent of such displaced workers made as much as or more than they did before being laid off; but for most workers, job loss is costly.[5]

Studies indicate that displaced workers' earnings may be lower for many years after their displacement. Workers displaced during the 1982 recession, for example, were earning 20 percent less, on average, than their nondisplaced peers 15 to 20 years later.[6] Displaced workers also experience greater earnings instability and subsequent periods of joblessness than other workers.[7]

In part, the poor outcomes for displaced workers might be attributable to the decline of employment in a particular industry or state, rather than, for example, the closure of a specific firm. Displaced workers tend to have previously held jobs in industries, states, and occupations where employment is falling as a result of changes in markets and technologies. Some of the earnings losses experienced by such workers probably reflect their inability to continue working in those declining industries, states, or occupations rather than to their separation from a particular employer.[8]

Job displacement, unemployment, and the attendant drop in earnings have serious effects on many families' overall finances. During the most recent recession, over half of the long-term unemployed withdrew money from their savings and retirement accounts to cover expenses; half had to borrow money from family and friends; and one-third had trouble meeting their housing expenses (including making mortgage or rent payments). Such outcomes can have adverse effects on family finances in the long term because of greater debt or depleted savings, higher interest payments (on borrowed money), forgone investment income, and higher tax bills (as a result of prematurely withdrawing money from a retirement account).[9]

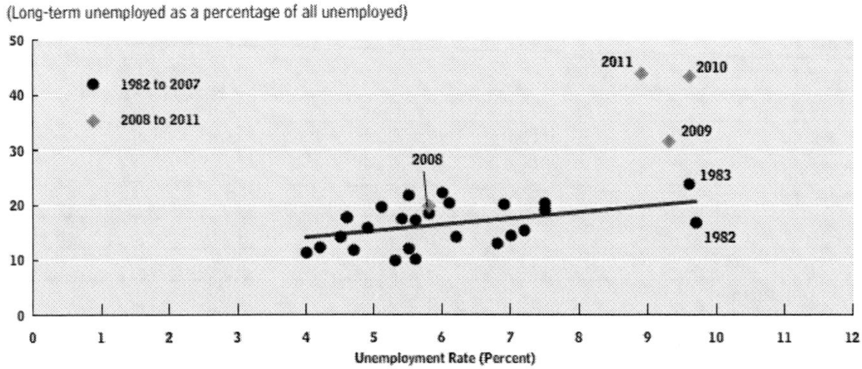

Source: Congressional Budget Office based on data from the Bureau of Labor Statistics.

Notes: The long-term unemployed have been unemployed for more than 26 weeks.

Data are based on the portion of the population ages 16 and older. The most recent recession began in December 2007 and ended in June 2009. The sloped line in the figure represents the historical relationship between the overall unemployment rate and the percentage of the unemployed who have been seeking work for more than 26 weeks, reflecting the individual observations that are shown in the figure for the years from 1982 to 2007. The points in the figure for 2009 through 2011 are far above that historical relationship.

Figure 2. Relationship Between the Unemployment Rate and the Long-Term Unemployed as a Share of All Unemployed, 1982 to 2011.

Table 1. Characteristics of the Labor Force and the Unemployed, March 2011

Percent	Labor Force	Unemployeda	Long-Term Unemployed
Sex			
Male	53	59	59
Female	47	41	41
Educational Attainment			
High school diploma or less	38	58	54
Some college	30	27	29
Bachelor's degree	21	12	12
Graduate degree	11	4	5
Marital Status			

Table 1. (Continued)

Percent	Labor Force	Unemployeda	Long-Term Unemployed
Not married	57	39	41
Married	43	61	59
Race or Ethnicity			
Caucasian	67	55	53
Hispanic	15	20	18
African American	11	19	22
Other	7	6	7
Industry			
Service	47	39	39
Manufacturing	10	10	12
Construction	7	14	12
Other	34	29	30
No industry history	1	8	8
Reason for Unemployment			
Lost job involuntarily	b	62	62
Reentered the labor force	b	23	25
Entered labor force for first time	b	8	8
Left job voluntarily	b	7	5
Age			
16 to 24	14	26	19
25 to 54	68	61	64
55 to 69	19	13	17
Region			
South	36	35	35
West	23	27	27
Midwest	22	21	21
Northeast	18	17	17

Source: Congressional Budget Office based on the March 2011 Current Population Survey.

Notes: The labor force comprises people ages 16 and older who have a job or who are jobless but available for work and actively seeking employment. The long-term unemployed have been unemployed for more than 26 weeks.

[a] People are not officially considered unemployed unless they are in the labor force.

[b] Categories do not apply to all people in the labor force.

Box 2. Programs That May Aid Unemployed People

The *unemployment insurance* (UI) program provides temporary, partial earnings replacement for eligible workers who have been laid off from their job. To qualify for benefits, unemployed people must have lost their job through no fault of their own and have sufficient recent work histories and sufficiently high earnings in their most recent job.

UI payments range from 30 percent to 50 percent of their previous earnings for up to 26 weeks. The federal government pays states to administer the program, funds benefits for certain groups of unemployed workers, and provides general guidelines and some restrictions on how states may operate their UI programs.

Each state sets its own eligibility requirements, determines the duration and amount of regular benefits, and specifies the payroll taxes that fund those programs.

During the recent recession and its aftermath, federal legislation enabled states to extend the duration of UI benefits to as many as 99 weeks, depending on each state's unemployment rate. In January 2012, more than half of the nation's unemployed were receiving UI benefits.[1]

Several other federal programs provide assistance aimed particularly at people with disabilities or low family income.[2]

The *Supplemental Nutrition Assistance Program* (SNAP, formerly known as Food Stamps) and *Temporary Assistance for Needy Families* (TANF) provide assistance to low-income families, regardless of their employment history.

More families have received those benefits since the start of the recent recession; and, under the American Recovery and Reinvestment Act of 2009, the value of SNAP benefits increased, providing an additional financial backstop to beneficiaries.

Medicaid is a joint federal and state program that pays for health care services for a variety of individuals with low income.[3] Health insurance options for the unemployed will increase in 2014, as a result of expanded eligibility for Medicaid and the availability of subsidized coverage through health insurance exchanges under the Affordable Care Act enacted in 2010.

Less government assistance is available for unemployed workers whose spell of unemployment lasts many years. Unemployment insurance eventually runs out, and federal support through TANF can be received for a maximum of five years.

Some of the long-term unemployed eventually qualify for disability benefits through the Social Security Disability Insurance program (wherein the amount of the benefit is based on the individual's prior earnings) or through the Supplemental Security Income program (which is available to people with low income who are elderly, blind, or disabled).[4] Most people who qualify for those two programs leave the labor force and do not return to it. Disability insurance recipients collect those benefits until they qualify for retirement benefits through the Social Security program.

[1] CBO estimated that in 2009, 30 percent of all UI benefits went to individuals in households with income less than twice the federal poverty threshold and that the poverty rate in that year would have been 1.1 percentage points higher had it not been for those benefits. See Congressional Budget Office, "Unemployment Insurance Benefits and Family Income of the Unemployed," attachment to a letter to the Honorable Jim McDermott (November 17, 2010).

[2] For discussion of unemployment insurance and other programs that might help reduce hardship during unemployment, see Congressional Budget Office, Losing a Job During a Recession, Issue Brief (April 2010).

[3] Medicaid and the Children's Health Insurance Program are important sources of coverage for the children of the unemployed, but Medicaid has not been an important source of coverage for unemployed workers themselves. See Karyn Schwartz and Sonya Streeter, Health Coverage for the Unemployed (Washington, D.C.: Kaiser Family Foundation, June 2011), www.kff.org/uninsured/8201.cfm.

[4] For additional information, see Congressional Budget Office, Social Security Disability Insurance: Participation Trends and Their Fiscal Implications, Issue Brief (July 2010); and Umar Moulta-Ali, Primer on Disability Benefits: Social Security Disability Insurance (SSDI) and Supplemental Security Income (SSI), CRS Report for Congress RL32279 (Congressional Research Service, January 6, 2012).

Lower Earnings for New Entrants

The effects of high unemployment on people entering the labor market for the first time may persist throughout their careers. Labor market entrants may face a prolonged search before landing a job, and prevailing wages for entry-level jobs may be lower because of limited demand for new workers. One recent study of white men who graduated from college between 1979 and 1989 found that graduating in a poor economy had a long-term negative impact on wages.[10]

Adverse Health Effects

In addition to the lasting impact on earnings, unemployment and job loss may take a toll on people's health. A review of 104 empirical studies that assessed the impact of unemployment concluded that the unemployed were physically and psychologically worse off than their employed counterparts.[11] People who lost their job were more likely than other workers to report being in fair or poor health and having stress-related health conditions such as depression, stroke, heart disease, or heart attacks. Further, a substantial minority of the long-term unemployed reported having trouble getting or paying for medical care.[12] Moreover, research suggests that the negative effects of job loss on health may reduce life expectancy.[13]

Family Stresses

People's anxiety about family finances and related issues rose sharply during the most recent recession and that anxiety has persisted in its aftermath, with heightened concerns about layoffs and reductions in wages, hours, or benefits.[14] That anxiety has affected the employed as well as the unemployed.

The loss of income and elevated levels of household stress associated with a parent's job loss, particularly if the period of unemployment is prolonged, can also have lasting effects on children. According to one study, about one in nine children lived with an unemployed parent in December 2009.[15] Some research suggests that children whose fathers lose a job are at elevated risk of problems related to personality and emotional development, as well as with interpersonal relationships.[16] Parental job loss and subsequent unemployment are also associated with poorer schooling outcomes for children.[17] Ultimately, children of displaced workers, on average, have poorer economic outcomes as adults than the children of otherwise similar workers who have never experienced job loss.[18]

Factors Causing High Unemployment

In December 2007, the unemployment rate was 5.0 percent. Four years later, in December 2011 (when CBO completed its most recent economic forecast), that rate was 8.5 percent. CBO has estimated that the three-and-ahalf percentage-point increase in the unemployment rate over that period could be attributed to four factors in the following amounts:

- Weak demand for goods and services as a result of the recession and its aftermath, which accounts for about two-and-a-half percentage points;
- Mismatches between the needs of employers and the skills and location of the unemployed, which account for about one-half of one percentage point;
- Incentives from extensions of unemployment insurance for people to stay in the labor force and continue searching for work, which account for about one-quarter of one percentage point; and
- Erosion of skills and the stigma attached to long-term unemployment—that is, employers' perception that people who have been unemployed for a long time would be low-quality workers—which together account for about one-quarter of one percentage point.

Thus, in CBO's judgment, roughly a third of the net increase in unemployment over that four-year period has stemmed from factors other than weak demand. Some evidence for those other causes comes from shifts in the relationship between the job vacancy rate (the ratio of job openings to the sum of job openings and employment) and the unemployment rate, which is known as the Beveridge Curve. An increase in the unemployment rate relative to the job vacancy rate may suggest that unemployed workers are facing unusual difficulties finding suitable employment among the available job opportunities.[19] One recent study indicates such a shift in the relationship depicted by the Beveridge Curve: Before the recession, a job vacancy rate of 3.0 percent was associated with an unemployment rate of 5.0 percent; but, as of June 2011, that same 3.0 percent job vacancy rate was associated with an unemployment rate of 6.4 percent.[20]

In that study, about 1 percentage point of the elevated unemployment rate was attributed to skill and locational mismatches, extended unemployment insurance, and other factors. That finding is consistent with CBO's estimate that about 1 percentage point of the increase in the unemployment rate can be attributed to factors other than weak current demand.

Weak aggregate demand is also the primary contributor to the increased average duration of unemployment; the incentives from the extensions of unemployment insurance benefits and changes in the characteristics of the unemployed played smaller roles.[21]

Weak Demand for Goods and Services

Most of the increase in unemployment during the past four years and its persistence at a high level have resulted from a cyclical decline in the demand for goods and services, which has, in turn, decreased employers' demand for workers. Under current law, the cyclical weakness in demand stemming from the recent recession and slow recovery is likely to persist for the next few years; this cyclical weakness will continue to elevate the unemployment rate, though by diminishing amounts, through 2017, CBO estimates.

That weak demand can be attributed to various factors. Household spending fell and has remained weak, dampened by a loss of household wealth, an extraordinary decline in labor's share of national income, a desire by families and businesses to reduce debt as well as tightened lending conditions, and increased uncertainty and pessimism—in part reflecting the poor state of the job market. Residential construction has been anemic, held down by overbuilding during the boom, by poor expectations for future house prices, and, to a lesser degree, by weak household formation—which, like households' uncertainty and pessimism, in part reflects the poor state of the job market. Cutbacks by state and local governments have left government employment about 1.7 percent lower at the end of 2011 than it was at the end of 2007, just prior to the recession.

Moreover, business investment plunged during the recession, as businesses reacted to a decline in aggregate demand, a very uncertain outlook, and tightening credit. Since the recession's end, growth in business investment has been a bright spot, relatively speaking, although business investment and hiring are still being restrained by businesses' expectations that aggregate demand will continue to grow only moderately. In addition, some businesses may be concerned about how they will be affected by the implementation of recently enacted legislation dealing with the financial system and health care, by the government's regulatory policies in other areas, and by possible future changes in federal tax and spending policies.[22] However, the degree to which each of those factors has restrained investment and hiring is difficult to determine.

Mismatches Between Employers' Needs and the Skills and Location of Workers

A distinctive feature of the U.S. labor market is its dynamism. Individual employers grow and shrink in response to changes in demand and business success, workers often change jobs as they seek out a position that best fits their skills and interests, and there are always shifts in the economy resulting from changes in technology, consumer preferences, and international trade, which have disproportionate effects on certain industries, occupations, and locations. The need for workers to shift from one industry or occupation to another, to acquire new skills to facilitate such a shift, or even to relocate in order to find a new job is often referred to as a skill or locational mismatch. Those factors mean that there will always be some unemployment—which has ranged from about 4 percent to 5 percent in recent decades—as firms with unfilled openings and workers looking for jobs sort themselves into the most productive matches. Economists refer to that type of unemployment as frictional and view it as an important information-gathering process that leads to improved matches between workers and employers (although government policies that facilitate or hindersuch matching can affect the amount of frictional unemployment).

Unemployment may temporarily rise when extraordinary changes in technology or in the demand for various products necessitate a change in the distribution of workers among industries, occupations, or locales. As an example, the advent of computerized word processing in the 1980s greatly reduced the need for typists and secretaries; consequently, many people in those occupations had to find other lines of work, and some employers had to search for workers skilled in the new technology. At such times, the magnitude of skill mismatch increases significantly relative to its historical average, boosting unemployment while those adjustments take place. Such adjustments can take months or years, and thus can contribute to longterm unemployment.

CBO estimates that an increase in skill and locational mismatches accounted for roughly half a percentage point of the increase in unemployment during and following the recent recession. That effect will diminish gradually over the next five years, in CBO's judgment, as people acquire new skills, shift to faster-growing indus tries and occupations, and relocate to take advantage of those opportunities.[23]

Table 2. Employment, by Industry, 2007 to 2011

	Number of Employees (Millions)		*Percentage Change,*
Industry	*2007*	*2011*	*2007–2011*
Construction	7.6	5.5	-28
Manufacturing	13.9	11.7	-16
Information	3.0	2.7	-12
Financial Activities	8.3	7.6	-8
Trade, Transportation, and Utilities	26.6	24.9	-6
Professional and			
Business Services	17.9	17.2	-4
Leisure and Hospitality	13.4	13.2	-2
Other Services	5.5	5.4	-1
Government	22.2	22.1	-1
Mining/Logging	0.7	0.8	9
Educational and Health Care Services	18.3	20.0	9

Source: Congressional Budget Office based on data from the Bureau of Labor Statistics.

Skill Mismatches

Although one source of such mismatches during the past few years has been the decline in demand for construction workers that followed the collapse of the housing market, two findings from analyses of the distribution of employment among industries support the conclusion that skill mismatches account for a small portion of the rise in unemployment. First, if workers' skills and the needs of growing industries were increasingly mismatched, workers laid off in declining industries should have a harder time finding new jobs than workers laid off in other industries. That has not been the case.[24] Second, because employment has declined in many industries, there are unemployed workers in most broad industry categories who have relevant skills and experience (see Table 2; educational and health care services is the only large industry showing employment gains). Nevertheless, shifts in the demand for labor could have occurred *within* broad industry categories. Although those facts do not rule out such industrial shifts as a partial explanation for elevated unemployment, developments affecting all industries are a more important part of the story.

Locational Mismatches

Locational mismatches have probably played a minor role in the rise of both unemployment and long-term unemployment, despite the fact that unemployment rates vary substantially among states. For example, in December 2011, the four states with the highest rates of unemployment—California, Nevada, Mississippi, and Rhode Island—all had unemployment rates exceeding 10 percent. The three states with the lowest rates of unemployment—Nebraska, North Dakota, and South Dakota—had rates below 5 percent. Although that dispersion in unemployment rates suggests locational mismatches between workers and labor demand, it is important to note that those latter three states have small populations and a very small share of the nation's jobs; in contrast, all 10 of the largest states currently have higher unemployment rates. Thus, national unemployment would not decline sharply even if unemployed workers flocked to states with the lowest rates of unemployment.

The severity of locational mismatches may be exacerbated if workers cannot relocate because they are unable to sell their houses. In historical terms, a large number of homeowners are "underwater"—that is, their houses are worth less than what they owe on their mortgages. Some analysts suggest that homeowners who are underwater may be unable to move to locales where labor demand is stronger and where they might find work. Whether that is occurring is unclear, however: Three recent studies arrive at disparate conclusions as to whether homeowners with negative equity have been less mobile than other homeowners.[25]

Incentives from Extensions of Unemployment Insurance

The UI system helps unemployed workers and their families in several ways. Most directly, the system provides income support to people who have lost their job for reasons other than poor performance or misconduct. Research has shown that UI helps recipients to maintain their standard of living after losing a job. Research also suggests that UI allows job seekers to take a more entrepreneurial career path—which can be productive but risky—than they would have taken in the absence of such insurance.[26]

UI also encourages laid-off workers to continue searching for work rather than leaving the labor force, because continued receipt of UI benefits requires them to be actively looking for work. That requirement to search for work results in some laid-off workers returning to work rather than leaving the workforce altogether. However, the availability of UI also discourages unemployed people from taking a job they might consider unsuitable because those benefits reduce the hardship of being unemployed. Economists have traditionally viewed that effect as significant. One widely cited study from 1990 found that eligibility for five extra weeks of benefits led to, on average, a one-week increase in the length of an unemployment spell.[27] More-recent studies have suggested, however, that only about 40 percent of that one-week increase in the duration of unemployment was the result of a diminished incentive to take a job; the remaining 60 percent of that increase represented an expanded search effort, which can ultimately result in better job matches.[28]

In addition, the availability of UI benefits affects the employment of prospective workers who are ineligible for benefits, such as those who are new entrants or reentrants to the labor force. For example, to the extent that people who are receiving benefits are less likely to accept available jobs, those who are not receiving benefits are more likely to obtain and accept job offers. Moreover, by putting money in the hands of people who spend much of it on goods and services, UI benefits increase the demand for workers needed to produce those goods and services, indirectly raising total employment compared with what it otherwise would be. Thus, the effects of UI benefits on overall employment and unemployment differ from their effects on the employment and unemployment of recipients alone.

Because of the various ways that UI benefits affect people's incentives and opportunities, analyzing the impact of the extensions of benefits (from the usual 26 weeks up to 99 weeks) during the recession and its aftermath is difficult. The extensions of benefits have had two types of effects:

- They have increased recipients' spending and, thus, the demand for goods and services in the economy as a whole, which has tended to raise employment and reduce unemployment. CBO estimates that the twoand-a-half percentage point increase in unemployment resulting from weak demand would have been greater without the extensions of benefits.
- At the same time, in order to remain eligible for unemployment benefits, more people without jobs have continued looking for work—though, in some cases, less intensely and more selectively than they otherwise would have—after the normal 26-week benefit period; in that way, the extensions of benefits have kept more jobless individuals in the labor force, thereby pushing up the unemployment rate by roughly one-quarter of one percentage point, CBO estimates.[29] (That

effect will dissipate shortly after those extensions end, whereas the effects of some of the other factors raising unemployment will last longer.)

Whether the combination of those two effects has raised or lowered the unemployment rate in total in the short term is unclear. In CBO's analysis, which encompassed a range of possible effects of UI extensions on demand and on people's choices about staying in the labor force, the two effects together could have either raised or lowered the unemployment rate. (According to that analysis, the UI extensions have raised total employment, which has been constrained principally by weak demand for labor.)

UI extensions also contributed to the increase in the proportion of unemployed people who have been seeking jobs for more than 26 weeks, in CBO's judgment. An important feature of the UI system is that only displaced workers are eligible for UI benefits; those who quit their job and people new to or reentering the labor force are generally not eligible. Thus, the disincentives to work stemming from the extensions of UI mainly affected displaced workers, particularly those who had already received benefits for 26 weeks. In fact, between 2008 and 2010, the percentage of long-term unemployed among people who had lost jobs rose much more than that percentage among people who became unemployed for reasons other than job loss (see Figure 3). A recent study analyzing such differences found that UI extensions during and after the recent recession elevated the share of long-term unemployment.[30]

"Stigma" and the Erosion of Skills

Regardless of its initial cause, unemployment in general and long-term unemployment in particular can lead to subsequent difficulties for the affected workers. One mechanism by which unemployment reduces future employment prospects is through the stigma attached to long-term unemployment—that is, an employer's inference that people who have been unemployed for a long time are low-quality workers. Long-term unemployment may also erode workers' skills, and those two factors— stigma and skill erosion—may have interactive effects. The extent to which stigma and skill erosion increased unemployment and long-term unemployment during and after the most recent recession is difficult to quantify. CBO estimates that those factors currently account for about a quarter of a percentage point of the increase in unemployment during and following the recession; CBO expects that effect to grow to about half a point during the next several years, and then to persist at that level for several more years before gradually diminishing.

Stigma

Prospective employers might interpret long-term unemployment as a negative signal about the worker's skills, motivation, and general employability.[31] When the unemployment rate is very high, however, employers may infer that a prospective worker's unemployment is attributable to overall economic conditions rather than to his or her own shortcomings. Some research, for example, found smaller stigma effects for workers who lost their job as a result of a plant closing rather than through a more selective layoff process.[32]

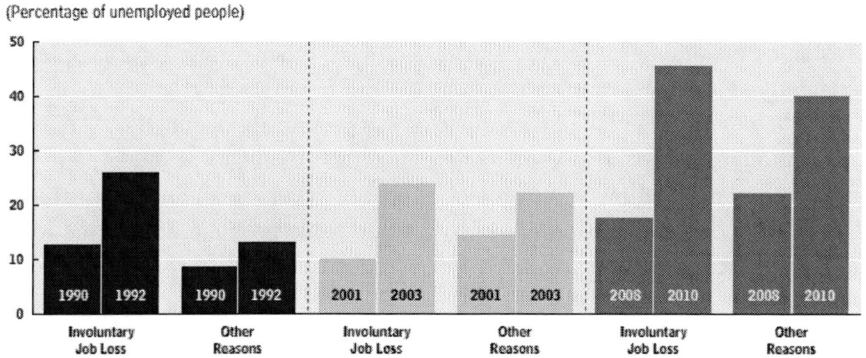

Source: Congressional Budget Office based on data from the Current Population Survey, Outgoing Rotation Groups.

Notes: The long-term unemployed have been unemployed for more than 26 weeks.

Data are based on the portion of the population ages 16 and older.

The category "other reasons" encompasses people who have reentered the labor force, entered the labor force for the first time, or left their previous job voluntarily.

The last three recessions in the United States spanned the following periods: July 1990 to to March 1991; March 2001 to November 2001; and December 2007 to June 2009.

Figure 3. Long-Term Unemployment During and Immediately Following Three Recent Recessions, by Reason for Unemployment.

Still, even if weak economic conditions lead to less stigma for any given duration of unemployment, stigma may be greater the longer a spell of unemployment lasts. Long-term unemployment may thus produce a self-perpetuating cycle wherein protracted spells of unemployment heighten employers' reluctance to hire those individuals, which in turn leads to even longer spells of joblessness.

Erosion of Skills

Workers acquire skills through on-the-job training or, more commonly, through work experi ence. Evidence that skills erode during periods of unemployment comes in part from studies on the negative effects that time out of the labor force has on wages.[33]

Skill erosion may take the form of lost familiarity with the technical aspects of an occupation, such as how to use particular computer programs or how to manipulate certain equipment. Skill erosion is particularly problematic when the technology used in an occupation changes regularly—in such instances, even unemployed workers who maintain their old skills may fall behind because they do not actively work with newer technologies. The erosion of people's productive capacity can take other forms; for example, an unemployed salesperson may lose contact with a particular client base or with the particular market niche in which he or she previously operated.

Although the specific knowledge that is lost or made obsolete varies by industry and occupation, some erosion probably occurs in all but the most low-skilled jobs, and the erosion of skills is a pervasive problem among the long-term unemployed.

Policies to Increase Demand for Workers

Policies that increase demand for workers address the single most important factor behind today's persistently high unemployment rates—weak demand for goods and services. CBO has previously assessed the potential impact of a variety of temporary fiscal policy actions that might promote economic growth and increase employment in the near term.[34] This section summarizes those earlier estimates and the agency's findings about other options that could affect the demand for workers.

Fiscal Policies

Each of the policy options that CBO previously analyzed would primarily affect the economy in one of three different ways:

- By boosting households' disposable income,
- By providing support to businesses, or
- By increasing aid to state governments or government spending on infrastructure.

Using evidence from empirical studies and econometric models, CBO assessed the impact of such policies on the nation's output (GDP) and total employment in 2012 and 2013 per million dollars of total budgetary cost (measured in terms of additional government spending or reduction in taxes). To encompass most economists' views about the effects of each type of policy, CBO used low and high estimates of the effects on output and employment. By CBO's estimates, the impact of the policies would range from a very small increase in employment to an increase of as much as 19 years of full-time- equivalent (FTE) employment per million dollars of budgetary cost over that two-year span (see Figure 4).

(An FTE-year is 40 hours of employment per week for one year.)

On the basis of that analysis, CBO concluded the following:

- Policies that would have the largest effects on employment per dollar of budgetary cost in 2012 and 2013 are those that would reduce the marginal cost to businesses of adding employees or that would target people most likely to spend the additional income. Such policies include reducing employers' payroll taxes (especially if limited to firms that increase their payroll), increasing aid to the unemployed, and providing additional refundable tax credits in 2012 for lower- and middle-income households; and
- Policies that would primarily affect businesses' cash flow but would have little impact on their marginal incentives to hire or invest would have only small effects. Such policies include reducing business income taxes and reducing tax rates on repatriated foreign earnings.

All of the options that CBO considered were sufficiently scalable—that is, able to be increased in size in an efficient manner—such that they could entail at least $10 billion in spending increases or tax cuts in 2012 and 2013.

The estimated effects of the policies on economic output varied from as little as 10 cents per dollar of budgetary cost to as much as $1.90 per dollar of budgetary cost. A rough rule-of-thumb applicable to the policies shown in Figure 4 would be the following: An additional $30 billion used in 2012 for an

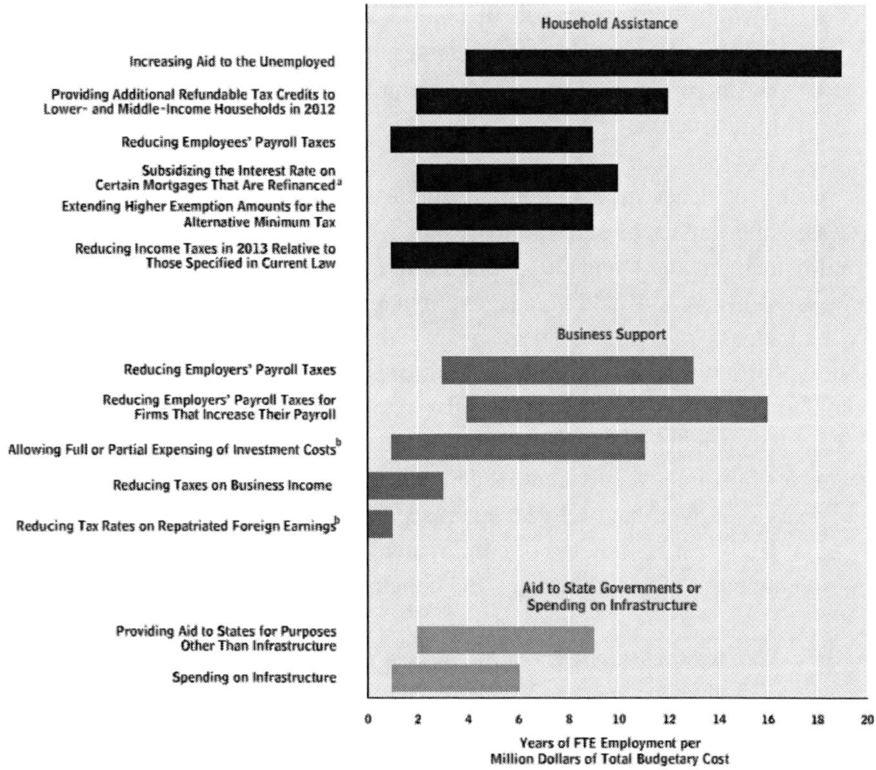

Source: Congressional Budget Office.

Notes: The ranges of estimates were chosen, on a judgmental basis, to encompass most economists' views. Estimates represent years of full-time-equivalent employment (FTE-years) with a given policy minus FTE-years without the policy. (An FTE-year is 40 hours of employment per week for one year.) Estimates are per million dollars of total budgetary cost, which is the amount of tax revenues or outlays over the full duration of a policy's effects, except as specified in note b below. All years are calendar years. Unless otherwise specified, increased spending authority was assumed to be available as of January 2012, and tax options were assumed to be in effect only for 2012.

[a]. Includes the effects of extending higher exemption amounts for the alternative minimum tax in 2012.

[b]. For this option, total budgetary cost is calculated as a discounted present value rather than as the sum of changes in tax revenues over the full duration of the policy's effects.

Figure 4. Ranges of Cumulative Effects of Policy Options on Employment in 2012 and 2013.

option that would boost employment in 2012 and 2013 by about 9 FTE-years per million dollars of total budgetary cost would translate into a reduction in the unemployment rate of one-tenth of one percentage point (say, at the beginning of 2013). Thus, changes in fiscal policy, if appropriately designed and large in scale, could substantially reduce unemployment during the next few years.[35]

Those policy actions would generally decrease FTE-years of unemployment by the same amount that they would increase FTE-years of employment, with the exception of the option of increasing benefits for unemployment insurance. In the current economic climate, extensions of UI benefits affect the labor market through some channels that tend to increase the number of employed people (such as by increasing demand for goods and services). However, such extensions also tend to increase the number of unemployed people (for example, because more jobless workers choose to remain in the labor force in order to receive benefits). Thus, the net effect of additional spending for unemployment insurance on the number of unemployed people is unclear.[36]

Policies not analyzed in CBO's previous work, such as direct government employment in public service jobs, could also reduce unemployment. The federal government hired millions of unemployed workers during the Great Depression through the Work Projects Administration and the Civilian Conservation Corps. More recently, under the American Recovery and Reinvestment Act, the federal government provided aid to states to place applicants to the Temporary Assistance to Needy Families (TANF) program in jobs.[37] It might be difficult, however, to efficiently and productively implement a program involving direct hiring on a scale at which spending would exceed $10 billion in 2012 and 2013—a criterion that CBO used when selecting policies to analyze in its previous work.

The fiscal policy approaches discussed above would increase total demand for workers, although some— such as tax credits for firms that expand payroll—could explicitly target the long-term unemployed. People who have been unemployed for a long time could still benefit from untargeted approaches even if most jobs directly created by the policies went to other groups.

Despite the near-term economic benefits that would arise from reductions in taxes and increases in government spending, such actions would add to the already large projected budget deficits that would exist under current policies, either immediately or over time. Unless offsetting actions were taken to reverse the accumulation of additional government debt, the nation's capital stock (that is, the tools, machines, and factories used in production), its future output, and people's future income would tend to be lower than they otherwise would have been. If policymakers wanted to boost the economy in the near term while seeking to achieve fiscal sustainability over the long term, a combination of policies would be required— specifically, changes in taxes and spending that would widen the deficit now but reduce it later in the decade. Such an approach would work best if the future policy changes were sufficiently specific and widely supported so that households, businesses, state and local governments, and participants in financial markets believed that the future fiscal restraint would truly take effect.

Other Types of Legislative Actions

Lawmakers could also influence the demand for workers during the next few years by changing policies that do not involve, or whose scope extends well beyond, taxation and government spending. For example, legislation could modify existing or proposed regulations, significantly alter the government's role in a particular sector of the economy, or change trade relationships with other countries. The near-term economic impact of changing a regulation or other policy—apart from fiscal policy—would depend importantly on how doing so affected businesses' investment and hiring decisions. In addition, changes in policies that increased or decreased households' purchasing power or wealth would affect how much they spend. Finally, changes to regulations and other policies could affect expectations about future income or make businesses and households more or less uncertain about future government policies and economic conditions, which would affect economic growth and employment in the near term.

CBO has previously discussed some potential changes in regulatory policies and other policies related to energy and the environment, the financial and health care sectors, and international trade.38 But estimating the near-term effects of such policy changes on overall economic activity is exceedingly difficult, and few analytic tools are available for that purpose. Accordingly, CBO did not attempt to quantify the effects of those potential changes with any precision. (Other types of policy changes that do not require legislation, such as those related to monetary policy or those that can be implemented by federal agencies under current law, could also affect economic activity, but they were outside the scope of that analysis.)

Table 3. Funding for Training Under the Workforce Investment Act (Title I), Fiscal Year 2012

	Funding in Billions of Dollars
State Formula Grant Programs	
Youth Activities Formula Grants	0.8
Adult Activities Formula Grants	0.8
Dislocated Worker Grants	1.2
Job Corps	1.7
National Programs	0.4
Total	4.9

Source: David H. Bradley, The Workforce Investment Act and the One-Stop Delivery System, CRS Report for Congress R41135 (Congressional Research Service, January 13, 2012).

Some of the changes in policies that CBO considered in its previous work would probably raise output and employment over the next few years; other changes would probably lower output and employment; and some changes would have effects on economic activity that are difficult to determine. However, in CBO's judgment, the economic effects of the specific changes in regulatory policies or other policies that the agency discussed in its previous work—apart from those related to fiscal policy—probably would be too small or would occur too slowly to significantly alter overall unemployment in the next two years. That analysis did not speak to other considerations that are critical when evaluating such policy changes, including their long-term effects on the economy, on people's health, and on the environment.

The policy changes that CBO examined were illustrative rather than exhaustive; many others, which might have larger or smaller economic effects, are possible. One such policy that CBO did not previously analyze would be a reduction in the minimum wage. Although estimates have varied, the bulk of the evidence indicates that such a reduction would increase employment by a small amount and correspondingly reduce unemployment by a small amount.[39] The effects would be largest for teenage and other low-skill workers whose wages are affected by the legal minimum. One factor limiting the potential effectiveness of such a policy, however, is that 41 states and the District of Columbia have their own minimum wages that are equal to or higher than the federal minimum (although they differ somewhat in their coverage of workers and in their enforcement); lowering the federal minimum would have little or no effect in those states. Also, current federal policy already makes some allowance for lower minimum wages for students and youths.

Other Policies to Reduce Unemployment

Other types of policies could aim to reduce unemployment by addressing factors other than weak aggregate demand for goods and services. The United States currently has numerous programs that aim to help job seekers in those ways. Some of those programs provide services—including job-search assistance, counseling, and training—through One-Stop Career Centers operated by state and local workforce-development agencies. For fiscal year 2012, the Congress has appropriated $4.9 billion for those services and other training activities under title I of the Workforce Investment Act of 1998, including the Job Corps and a variety of grants to states (see Table 3). In addition to those dedicated funds, the federal government spends $10 billion to $12 billion per year on other training programs, though there is some overlap and administrative inefficiency in those programs.[40]

Relative to the size of the workforce, the United States spends far less on formal training programs for the unemployed than most other industrialized nations.[41] However, a considerable amount of federal financial support is available for individuals pursuing training through community colleges and through certain proprietary education and training organizations.[42] Among existing programs that aim to help job seekers, some appear to have generated high rates of return for some groups, but others have had no impact and may, indeed, have had harmful effects.[43]

CBO has examined a number of policies that would focus on the unemployed and long-term unemployed in one of the following three ways:

- Improving the skills of unemployed workers,
- Modifying unemployment insurance to provide continued support to the long-term unemployed or to encourage the unemployed to take new jobs quickly and retain their work skills, or
- Facilitating transitions to work.

CBO has not estimated the effects on employment of any specific policy. The impact on employment per dollar of budgetary cost for those policies would probably be within the broad range of effects for the fiscal policies discussed earlier. But another important consideration for understanding the effects of such policies involves their potential scale; for many of those activities, spending tens of billions of additional dollars in 2012 and 2013 would be difficult. For that reason, their potential impact on the unemployment rate during the next two years is limited.

Many of the policies that CBO examined for this chapter would involve collaboration between the federal government and states or other entities. Key elements of the policies include the funding mechanism, the amount of funding, and the program design. The extent to which federal policymakers would influence the specific design of the programs would depend on the details of the legislation and the funding mechanism. (For a discussion of funding mechanisms, see Box 3).

Improving Workers' Skills

Training programs—including those designed to develop general workforce skills and programs that target specific industries and occupations in specific locations—could make the long-term unemployed more attractive to employers by addressing skills mismatch, skill erosion, and stigma. The benefits of training programs depend on the skills unemployed workers already have and their work experience. Unemployed high school dropouts might benefit greatly from basic skills training, whereas more-highly skilled workers might be better served by specialized training. The higher earnings from better training for young people accrue for many years and are more likely to exceed the investment cost; investment returns would probably be lower for older workers with fewer years before retirement.

General Workforce Programs

Well-designed training programs improve the employment and earnings outcomes of properly targeted participants, at least in the short run, and can lead to higher output. Training programs funded under the Job Training Partnership Act of 1982 had positive effects on adult participants' earnings (relative to a control group) for up to four years following training.[44] The extent to which the training approaches studied might work for the long-term unemployed, however, is unclear. Those who benefited the most from the training were those with the least skills and work experience. Because many of the long-term unemployed have work experience and basic job skills, they may need higher-level training to obtain new jobs that pay more than entry-level wages.

Sectoral Programs

Postsecondary education and training programs that target local employers' specific needs have had positive results for participants. For example, according to one study, additional education and training at community colleges that led to degrees or certificates contributed to economic gains for displaced workers who were unlikely to return to their previous occupations and industries.[45]

Sectoral employment programs have grown in prominence in recent years, and well-run programs have successfully placed participants in jobs and improved both wage rates and annual earnings.[46] Sectoral employment programs work with employers in narrow geographic areas (at the county level, for instance) to identify hiring needs in specific industries and occupations. The programs then develop training curricula to prepare the target population—the unemployed and those who left the labor force specifically to pursue training—for the jobs available in the area. Examples of successful sectoral training programs include those that have focused on:

- Medical and basic office skills and computerized accounting;
- Information technology and computer recycling and refurbishing; and
- Health care, manufacturing, and certain types of construction jobs (road construction and the abatement of lead and other hazardous materials).

Although some sectoral training programs have enjoyed success, practitioners are still learning how to best operate such programs, and it is unclear whether the programs can be applied on a sufficiently comprehensive scale to significantly reduce unemployment and aid the longterm unemployed nationwide, particularly in the next two years.

Programs Focused on Youth

Special policies may be needed to deal with unemployment and long-term unemployment among young workers. Overall unemployment rates are highest for the young, especially teenagers (23.2 percent in January 2012, as compared with an overall rate of 8.3 percent), and many young people are among the long-term unemployed. Policies that improve schooling and training options for young people— particularly those from low-income families—can enhance their future employment prospects. Potential approaches include the expanded use of career academies and programs such as the National Guard Youth Challenge for high-school-age youth and Registered Apprenticeship programs and Year Up for older youth.

Box 3. Funding Mechanisms

If federal lawmakers wanted to address unemployment by improving workers' skills, modifying the unemployment insurance program, or facilitating transitions to work, they could use various types of funding mechanisms to support those efforts.[1]

- Block grants typically give states broad flexibility to use funds to tailor programs to local conditions. For example, the Community Services Block Grant program, which is administered by the Department of Health and Human Services, provides states with funding for local entities that offer services and sponsor activities addressing employment, education, household budgeting, housing, nutrition, emergency services, and health.
- Categorical formula grants are directed to specified activities. For example, funding for the training of displaced workers is currently provided to states as a categorical grant; the formula allocating funds depends on states' shares of overall unemployment and long-term unemployment and on other factors. Categorical grants are sometimes structured to require state matching funds or to reimburse states for qualifying activities.
- Categorical project grants are generally awarded on the basis of a particular proposal's perceived merits. For instance, the Trade Adjustment Assistance Community College and Career Training Grants Program, which is administered by the Department of Labor, competitively awards grants of this type to institutions of higher learning that provide services to certain displaced workers.
- Federal operation of programs typically involves direct federal contact with participating entities, rather than partnership with state and local governments. The Job Corps, for example, provides training opportunities to low-income youth, and the Department of Labor directly contracts with participating institutions on behalf of eligible clients.

The different funding mechanisms entail different degrees of federal involvement. The role of the federal government in selecting, implementing, and overseeing the various programs is typically limited when those programs are funded through block grants and much more extensive for direct operation. That role can vary greatly for programs funded through categorical formula or project grants, depending on how the authorizing legislation is written.[2]

1. For further discussion of these approaches, see Shama Gamkhar, Federal Intergovernmental Grants and the States: Managing Devolution (United Kingdom: Edward Elgar Publishing, 2002).
2. See Harry J. Holzer, "Raising Job Quality and Skills for American Workers: Creating More-Effective Education and Workforce Development Systems in the States," Brookings Hamilton Project Discussion Paper 2011-10 (November 2011), www.brookings.edu/papers/2011/11_workforce _holzer.aspx.

Career academies are small learning communities of high school students that combine academic and technical curricula with a focus on specific careers. Career academies were first developed some 35 years ago, and the approach is currently used in an estimated 2,500 high schools. Evaluations of career academies found lasting positive effects on participants admitted to the program through a lottery process in comparison with a group of equally qualified applicants who were not admitted through that same process. For example, one study found that, four years after graduation, young men from low-income families who participated in the academies had worked an average of about three months more than their nonparticipating peers.[47]

The National Guard Youth ChalleNGe program targets high school dropouts between the ages of 16 and 18 who are not heavily involved with the justice system and who are drug-free. The program provides education and service experience to participants in a residential, quasi-military setting for 20 weeks, along with a year of mentoring after the residential component has been completed. Established in 1993, the program has about 100,000 graduates. Evaluations of the program indicate that participants earned GEDs and high school degrees at far higher rates than a similar group of nonparticipants. Those who participated in the program were also more likely to be employed and have higher earnings than their peers who had not participated.[48]

Registered Apprenticeship programs coordinated by the Department of Labor provide specific job and trade skills to participants through work-based learning and academic instruction. About half a million people participate in Registered Apprenticeship programs in the United States, proportionately far less than in other industrialized countries, such as Austria and Germany.[49] Some research suggests that the employment and earnings gains associated with apprenticeship programs exceed those of training obtained through community colleges and under the Workforce Investment Act.[50] Because the federal role has been limited to coordination of Registered Apprenticeship programs (federal funding was $28 million in 2011), a policy that substantially expanded federal support might require greater federal involvement and oversight.

Year Up—a private, nonprofit program—targets young people ages 18 to 24 and provides six months of technical skills training and classes in business writing and communication, followed by a six-month internship with a sponsoring company. Participants are paid a weekly stipend. In 2011, the program enrolled about 1,400 students in nine cities. An evaluation of the program found that although participants were no more likely than their peers to be working a year after completing the program, when they did work, their earnings were about 30 percent higher.[51]

Modifying Unemployment Insurance

Changes to the unemployment insurance program that encourage unemployed people to return to work quickly, that keep the unemployed connected to the workplace, and that even forestall job loss could reduce persistently high unemployment in the future. (Other types of changes could have different effects.) Although some changes could be implemented quickly, several years would probably be needed to fully implement most large changes—in part because of the multiple levels of government involved in the program. Possible changes to the UI program could include the following:

- Extending the duration of unemployment insurance benefits;
- Awarding reemployment bonuses to people who find a job quickly;
- Providing personal reemployment accounts with funds for people to purchase services that help them find a job;
- Offering wage insurance payments to people who accept a job that pays less than their previous job;
- Using UI benefits to temporarily place the unemployed in jobs with private-sector employers;

- Supplementing the earnings of workers who, instead of being laid off, are offered reduced hours (commonly referred to as short-time compensation, or STC); and
- Targeting more services to people projected to have difficulty finding a job.

Extending Unemployment Insurance Benefits

Emergency benefits for people unemployed more than 26 weeks will expire beginning in March 2012. A policy that extended those benefits would increase demand for goods and services, but it would also tend to discourage some people from taking jobs and thereby losing their benefits. Hence, it would slow the matching of some people to jobs and thus cause further erosion in the skills of some people with long spells of unemployment. Such a policy would cause some jobless workers to choose to remain in the labor force to receive benefits, perhaps turning down a job they consider unsuitable (thus tending to *increase* unemployment). But it would also result in some other jobless workers taking those jobs and, by boosting demand for goods and services, increase overall employment (thus tending to *reduce* unemployment). Because of those and other factors discussed above, extending unemployment insurance benefits, on net, has boosted employment, but its net effect on unemployment is unclear. Unlike the other policies considered in this section, a large-scale extension of benefits could be implemented quickly.

Reemployment Bonuses

Policies that provide financial incentives for the unemployed to accept a job can reduce overall unemployment and guard against long-term unemployment. Reemployment bonuses are one-time payments to the unemployed who find work within a specified period of time after losing their job. Experiments with reemployment bonuses in the 1980s and 1990s provided mixed evidence regarding whether they reduced the number of weeks that unemployed workers received UI benefits.[52] The goal underlying such bonuses is to forestall long-term unemployment among the newly unemployed rather than to provide inducements for the long-term unemployed to go back to work. In fact, if reemployment bonuses were offered only to the longterm unemployed, they could paradoxically induce the newly jobless to stay unemployed until they qualified for bonus payments.

Although not technically reemployment bonuses, employment retention bonuses for the long-term unemployed have been used in the United Kingdom with great success. Under the U.K. Employment Retention and Advancement (ERA) program, the long-term unemployed who found jobs received a retention bonus amounting to £400 (approximately $600) every four months for up to two years as long as they continued working for at least 30 hours a week and for 13 weeks out of every 17.[53] Participants also received postemployment counseling, tuition assistance, and additional bonuses for training. The long-term unemployed who participated in the program had significantly higher employment rates and earnings than nonparticipants over the entire five-year study period. Further, the cost to the government of providing ERA bonuses to the long-term unemployed was less than the projected cost of providing standard assistance and services available to those people.

Personal Reemployment Accounts

Personal reemployment accounts are self-managed accounts, typically offered to people who are projected to exhaust their UI benefits. In 2004, eight states provided $3,000 to selected UI recipients and allowed them to use the funds as a reemployment bonus or for other reemployment services.[54] In a related initiative in 2006, eight states provided $3,000 per year for two years to fund personal reemployment accounts for selected UI recipients. Those recipients were encouraged to use those accounts to pursue training.[55] Although the effect of those accounts on recipients was not formally evaluated, they resemble earlier individual training accounts that were found to have little impact either on the amount of training received or on other outcomes in comparison with typical services provided in One-Stop centers that involve some counseling.[56] However, the labor market was stronger during that demonstration than it is today, and such accounts might be more effective in the weak labor market conditions projected for the next few years.

Wage Insurance

Unemployed workers may be reluctant to take a job paying less than they previously earned. Wage insurance provides reemployed workers some or all of the difference between their old wages and their new wages for a certain period, say two years. In the mid-1990s, five Canadian cities tried implementing wage insurance programs that offered new UI claimants 75 percent of the difference in wages for two years if they accepted a new job paying less than their previous job. However, the wage insurance programs appeared to have little effect on the length of time that unemployed workers continued to receive UI benefits in Canada.[57]

Temporary Unpaid Work for UI Recipients

If unemployment insurance was used to subsidize temporary work, the unemployed might be able to better maintain basic job skills and, at the same time, gain experience in a new industry or occupation. Employers could also benefit from the work done by those temporary employees— whom they would not be paying—and from the opportunity to evaluate prospective employees in the workplace. By maintaining and potentially enhancing the skills of the unemployed, and by bringing workers and employers together, such programs could reduce unemployment. One example of such a program is Georgia Works, which seeks to provide work experience to people receiving unemployment compensation. That program has not been formally evaluated.

Short-Time Compensation

Short-time compensation provides UI benefits to workers who, instead of being laid off, are offered the opportunity to work reduced hours by their employer. The traditional UI system provides benefits only to workers who have been laid off, thereby creat ing an incentive for firms to reduce the amount of labor they use through layoffs rather than reduced hours. By providing UI benefits to those who have their hours cut, STC motivates firms to retain more workers at fewer average hours per week, potentially reducing layoffs. There is evidence suggesting that European nations, such as Germany, avoided some of the run-up in unemployment experienced in the United States because of more widespread use of STC policies.[58]

Although 20 states operated STC programs embedded within their overall UI programs in 2011, those programs are not widely used.[59] Potential claimants may be unaware of the programs if they are not widely publicized by the states. One disadvantage of such programs is that short-time work may be uneconomical for workers who have lengthy commutes or other fixed costs associated with employment and also for employers who may have to continue paying full benefits to workers that they otherwise would have laid off. Also, STC is currently designed to be an alternative to temporary or seasonal layoffs, wherein firms expect to recall laid-off workers after several months. However, temporary layoffs are increasingly uncommon—in part because of the longterm decline in the share of employment in unionized and manufacturing firms, where temporary layoffs have been historically common.

Some potential advantages of STC programs—particularly in a recession when firms are uncertain about demand for their services or products—are that firms and workers gain time to make adjustments while maintaining valuable human capital. For example, if a firm is not able to return to its previous full-time employment level, natural attrition may make it possible to increase the hours of remaining employees over time, even if the total hours needed are permanently lower. For workers, the losses caused by reduced work are spread across a larger group of people rather than being concentrated on people who have been laid off. Further, workers may use the adjustment time to find new work, avoiding some or all of the potential permanent wage losses associated with layoffs.[60]

Targeted Services

Over the past two decades, states have experimented with policies that provide extra services to those UI recipients projected to be most likely to exhaust their benefits. Under such policies, states use statistical models to predict who is likely to remain unemployed for 26 or more weeks, and they then require those workers to participate in special job-search assistance programs as a condition of receiving UI benefits. Research suggests that such a policy, when well-targeted, can reduce the duration of unemployment, reduce UI expenditures, and improve the postunemployment earnings of UI recipients.[61] However, over the past decade, states have increasingly allowed UI claimants to make initial and continuing claims over the phone and via the Internet, which has reduced the chances that those claimants will receive job-search assistance and other reemployment services.[62]

Facilitating Transitions to Employment

Some unemployed people may be unable or unwilling to take advantage of available job opportunities, and certain policies could facilitate the transition to employment. People may not have information about available jobs or the skills to search effectively for them. They may also have to contend with the stigma resulting from long-term unemployment or immobility arising from housing constraints.

Job-Search Assistance

Among the services offered by One-Stop Career Centers are group workshops that focus on job-search techniques and access to computerized job listings. For workers who fail to find a job quickly, those centers may offer additional higher-cost services that include individualized counseling and, if other methods fail, vouchers for training programs. Findings from five demonstrations indicated that various combinations of job-search assistance and increased emphasis on work-search rules were effective in reducing unemployment.[63]

Skill Certification Programs

Skill certification programs can allay employers' concerns about whether the longterm unemployed are capable of being productive employees. Pure skill certification programs provide the unemployed with an opportunity to demonstrate their abilities to employers and thereby reduce the stigma of long-term unemployment.[64] That approach, of course, works best if the unemployed have the skills that prospective employers need. One example of a certification program for preexisting skills is the WorkKeys Career Readiness Certification used by a variety of states, including Indiana, North Carolina, and Virginia. WorkKeys offers certification in a variety of areas, including reading, applied math, business writing, and applied technology. Such programs allow the unemployed to obtain skill certification without going through lengthy training programs.

Housing Mobility Assistance

Helping the unemployed relocate might also reduce unemployment. However, recent federal housing policies aimed at helping people stay in their homes, while having various beneficial effects on people's lives, could result in fewer people moving to areas where jobs might be more plentiful. Numerous efforts have been undertaken since 2008 to assist homeowners who are underwater on their mortgages (that is, who owe more on their mortgages than their homes are currently worth); those efforts have occurred largely through the auspices of the Making Home Affordable (MHA) program. The Emergency Homeowners' Loan Program provided further loan relief specifically targeted to the unemployed. Those programs have been varied in their goals and, in the case of the largest (the $8 billion Hardest Hit Fund), have varied from state to state in their implementation. But their general goal has been to keep homeowners in their houses through mortgage modifications or assistance rather than to facilitate their move to a new location. MHA programs designed to facilitate short sales (when a homeowner sells his or her house for less than the mortgage amount owed) probably do make it easier for people to relocate, but those programs are small in relation to the majority of MHA programs that seek to keep homeowners in their homes.

End Note for Summary

[1]. See the statement of Douglas W. Elmendorf, Director, Congressional Budget Office, before the Senate Committee on the Budget, Policies for Increasing Economic Growth and Employment in 2012 and 2013 (November 15, 2011).

End Notes

[1]. There are two approaches to measuring the duration of unemployment in the Current Population Survey, which is the basis for official U.S. unemployment statistics. The first and more widely used method, which the Bureau of Labor Statistics used to produce the figures reported here, relies on respondents' retrospective characterization of how long they have been unemployed as of the survey date. An alternative approach relies on changes in respondents' characterizations of their labor force status between consecutive months. That approach yields different measures of the average duration of unemployment. For many respondents, the two approaches yield mutually inconsistent information. For further discussion, see Michael W. L. Elsby, Bart Hobijn, and Aysegul Sahin, The Labor Market in the Great Recession: An Update, Working Paper 2011-29 (Federal Reserve Bank of San Francisco, October 2011), www.frbsf.org/publications/ economics/papers/2011/wp11-29bk.pdf.

[2]. See Michael W. L. Elsby, Bart Hobijn, and Aysegul Sahin, "The Labor Market in the Great Recession," Brookings Papers on Economic Activity, vol. 41, no. 1 (Spring 2010), pp. 1–65, www.brookings.edu/economics/bpea/past-editions.aspx; and Michael W. L. Elsby, Bart Hobijn, and Aysegul Sahin, "Updates of a Selection of Figures from Elsby, Hobijn, and Sahin (2010)" (March 2011), www.ny.frb.org/research/economists/sahin/ pub.html.

[3]. Some evidence suggests that average physical health in the population as a whole may improve during recessionary times, in part because of reduced consumption of alcohol and tobacco. See Christopher J. Ruhm, "Healthy Living in Hard Times," Journal of Health Economics, vol. 24, no. 2 (March 2005), pp. 341–363; and Christopher J. Ruhm, "Good Times Make You Sick," Journal of Health Economics, vol. 22, no. 4 (July 2003), pp. 637–658.

[4]. See Bureau of Labor Statistics, "Worker Displacement, 2007–2009" (August 26, 2010), www.bls.gov/news.release/ disp.nr0.htm.

[5]. See Congressional Budget Office, Losing a Job During a Recession, Issue Brief (April 2010).

[6] See Till von Wachter, Jae Song, and Joyce Manchester, "Long-Term Earnings Losses Due to Mass Layoffs During the 1982 Recession: An Analysis Using U.S. Administrative Data from 1974 to 2004" (draft, Columbia University, April 2009), www.columbia.edu/ ~vw2112.

[7]. See Ann Huff Stevens, "Persistent Effects of Job Displacement: The Importance of Multiple Job Losses," Journal of Labor Economics, vol. 15, no. 1, part 1 (January 1997), pp. 165–188.

[8]. See William J. Carrington, "Wage Losses for Displaced Workers: Is It Really the Firm that Matters?" Journal of Human Resources, vol. 28, no. 3 (Summer 1993), pp. 435-462; and Derek Neal, "Industry-Specific Human Capital: Evidence from Displaced Workers," Journal of Labor Economics, vol. 13, no. 4 (October 1995), pp. 653–677.

[9]. See Paul Taylor and others, The Impact of Long-Term Unemployment: Lost Income, Lost Friends—and Loss of Self-Respect (Washington, D.C.: Pew Research Center, July 22, 2010), http://pewresearch.org/pubs/1674/poll-impact-long-termunemployment.

[10]. See Lisa Kahn, "The Long-Term Labor Market Consequences of Graduating from College in a Bad Economy," Labour Economics, vol. 17, no. 2 (April 2010), pp. 303–316.

[11] See Frances McKee-Ryan and others, "Psychological and Physical Well-Being During Unemployment: A Meta-Analytic Study," Journal of Applied Psychology, vol. 90, no. 1 (January 2005), pp. 53–76.

[12]. See Taylor and others, The Impact of Long-Term Unemployment: Lost Income, Lost Friends—and Loss of Self-Respect.

[13] See David J. Roelfs and others, "Losing Life and Livelihood: A Systematic Review and Meta-Analysis of Unemployment and All-Cause Mortality," Social Science and Medicine, vol. 72, no. 6 (March 2011), pp. 840–854.

[14] See Steven J. Davis and Till Von Wachter, "Recessions and the Costs of Job Loss" (draft, Columbia University, November 2011), www.columbia.edu/~vw2112; and Cliff Zukin, Carl Van Horn, and Charley Stone, Out of Work and Losing Hope: The Misery and Bleak Expectations of American Workers, Heldrich Center for Workforce Development of Rutgers University (September 2011), www.heldrich.rutgers.edu/news-updates/all/out-work-and-losinghope-misery-and-bleak-expectations-american-workers.

[15] See Phillip Lovell and Julia B. Isaacs, Families of the Recession: Unemployed Parents and Their Children (Washington, D.C.: First Focus Campaign for Children, June 2010), www.brookings.edu/ papers/2010/0114_families_recession_isaacs.aspx.

[16] See Vonnie C. McLoyd, "Socialization and Development in a Changing Economy: The Effects of Paternal Job and Income Loss on Children," American Psychologist, vol. 44, no. 2 (February 1989), pp. 293–302.

[17] See Ann Huff Stevens and Jessamyn Schaller, "Short-Run Effects of Parental Job Loss on Children's Academic Achievement," Economics of Education Review, vol. 30, no. 2 (April 2011), pp. 289– 299; and Ariel Kalil and Patrick Wightman, "Parental Job Loss and Children's Educational Attainment in Black and White Middle-Class Families," Social Science Quarterly, vol. 92, no. 1 (March 2011), pp. 57–78.

[18] See Philip Oreopoulos, Marianne Page, and Ann Huff Stevens, "The Intergenerational Effects of Worker Displacement," Journal of Labor Economics, vol. 26, no. 3 (July 2008), pp. 455–483.

[19] See, for example, remarks by Narayana Kocherlakota, president of the Federal Reserve Bank of Minneapolis, "Inside the FOMC" (presented in Marquette, Michigan, August 17, 2010), www.minneapolisfed.org/news_events/pres/ speech_display.cfm?id=4525.

[20] See Mary Daly and others, A Rising Natural Rate of Unemployment: Transitory or Permanent? Working Paper 2011-05 (Federal Reserve Bank of San Francisco, September 2011), www.frbsf.org/ publications/economics/papers/2011/wp11-05bk.pdf.

[21] See Rob Valletta and Katherine Kuang, Why Is Unemployment Duration So Long? Economic Letter 2012-03 (Federal Reserve Bank of San Francisco, September 2011), www.frbsf.org/ publications/economics/letter/2012/el2012-03.pdf.

[22] See Scott Baker, Nick Bloom, and Steven J. Davis, Has Economic Policy Uncertainty Hampered the Recovery? Chicago Booth Research Paper 12-06 (University of Chicago, February 2012).

[23] See Congressional Budget Office, The Budget and Economic Outlook: An Update (August 2011), p. 46. This estimate is roughly in line with other recent calculations; for example, see Aysegul Sahin and others, "Measuring Mismatch in the U.S. Labor Market" (draft, Federal

Reserve Bank of New York, October 2011), www.ny.frb.org/research/economists/sahin/papers.html. That research found that mismatches related to industry and occupation were substantial and those related to geography were not.

[24] See Elsby, Hobijn, and Sahin, The Labor Market in the Great Recession.

[25] See Fernando Ferreira, Joseph Gyourko, and Joseph Tracy, "Housing Busts and Household Mobility," Journal of Urban Economics, vol. 68, no. 1 (July 2010), pp. 34–45; Sam SchulhoferWohl, Negative Equity Does Not Reduce Homeowners' Mobility, Working Paper 682 (Federal Reserve Bank of Minneapolis, December 2010), www.minneapolisfed.org/publications_papers/ pub_display.cfm?id=4598; and Fernando Ferreira, Joseph Gyourko, and Joseph Tracy, Housing Busts and Household Mobility: An Update, Staff Report 526 (Federal Reserve Bank of New York, November 2011), http://newyorkfed.org/research/staff_reports/ sr526.html.

[26] See Daron Acemoglu and Robert Shimer, "Productivity Gains from Unemployment Insurance," European Economic Review, vol. 44, no. 7 (June 2000), pp. 1195–1224.

[27] See Lawrence F. Katz and Bruce D. Meyer, "The Impact of the Potential Duration of Unemployment Benefits on the Duration of Unemployment," Journal of Public Economics, vol. 41, no. 1 (February 1990), pp. 45–72. For more recent evidence, see David Card and Phillip B. Levine, "Extended Benefits and the Duration of UI Spells: Evidence from the New Jersey Extended Benefit Program," Journal of Public Economics, vol. 78, no. 1-2 (October 2000), pp. 107–138.

[28] For example, see Raj Chetty, "Moral Hazard Versus Liquidity and Optimal Unemployment Insurance," Journal of Political Economy, vol. 116, no. 2 (April 2008), pp. 173–234.

[29]. For other recent estimates of the direct effects of unemployment insurance on unemployment rates (apart from indirect effects on labor demand), see Jesse Rothstein, "Unemployment Insurance and Job Search in the Great Recession" (draft, University of California at Berkeley, October 2011), http://gsppi.berkeley.edu/ faculty/jrothstein/workingpapers/Rothstein-UI-Oct2011.pdf; and, see Henry S. Farber and Robert Valetta, "Extended Unemployment Insurance and Unemployment Duration in the Great Recession: The U.S. Experience" (draft, Princeton University, June 2011), www.irs.princeton.edu/sites/irs/files/event/uploads/ HenryFarber112811.pdf.

[30] See Robert Valletta and Katherine Kuang, Extended Unemployment and UI Benefits, Economic Letter 2010-12 (Federal Reserve Bank of San Francisco, April 2010), www.frbsf.org/publications/ economics/letter/2010/el2010-12.html.

[31] For additional information, see Equal Employment Opportunity Commission, "EEOC to Examine Treatment of Unemployed Job Seekers" (transcript of meeting held February 16, 2011), www.eeoc.gov/eeoc/meetings/2-16-11/index.cfm.

[32] See Robert Gibbons and Lawrence F. Katz, "Layoffs and Lemons," Journal of Labor Economics, vol. 9, no. 4, (October 1991), pp. 351-380; and Martin Biewen and Susanne Steffes, "Unemployment Persistence: Is There Evidence for Stigma Effects?" Economic Letters, vol. 106, no. 3 (March 2010), pp. 188–190.

[33]. See Marianne Bertrand, Claudia Goldin, and Lawrence F. Katz, "Dynamics of the Gender Gap for Young Professionals in the Financial and Corporate Sectors," American Economic Journal: Applied Economics, vol. 2, no. 3 (July 2010), pp. 228–255.

[34] See the statement of Douglas W. Elmendorf, Director, Congressional Budget Office, before the Senate Committee on the Budget, Policies for Increasing Economic Growth and Employment in 2012 and 2013 (November 15, 2011).

[35] A recent example of a large-scale fiscal policy action is the American Recovery and Reinvestment Act of 2009 (ARRA), which by CBO's estimate will ultimately have a

budgetary cost of about $825 billion, reduced the unemployment rate in 2010 by between 0.4 and 1.8 percentage points. See Congressional Budget Office, Estimated Impact of the American Recovery and Reinvestment Act on Employment and Economic Output from July 2011 Through September 2011 (November 2011).

[36] According to CBO's low estimate, which incorporates a smaller effect on demand and a larger effect on people's choices about staying in the labor force, an extension of UI benefits would cause unemployment to increase. Conversely, according to the agency's high estimate, which incorporates a larger effect on demand and a smaller effect on people's choices about staying in the labor force, UI extension would cause unemployment to decrease.

[37] In the year and a half that those funds were available, 39 states and several territories used $1.3 billion to create short-term subsidized jobs, roughly equally divided between summer jobs for youth and jobs for adults. See LaDonna Pavetti, Liz Schott, and Elizabeth Lower-Basch, Creating Subsidized Employment Opportunities for Low-Income Parents: The Legacy of the TANF Emergency Fund (Washington, D.C.: Center on Budget and Policy Priorities, February 2011), www.cbpp.org/cms/index.cfm?fa=view& id=3400.

[38] Those policies include the approval process for energy projects, regulations regarding emissions from coal-burning power plants, the Dodd-Frank Wall Street Reform and Consumer Protection Act (Public Law 111-203), the Affordable Care Act (P.L. 111- 148), and free-trade agreements. See Congressional Budget Office, Policies for Increasing Economic Growth and Employment in 2012 and 2013, pp. 44–52.

[39] See David Card and Alan B. Krueger, Myth and Measurement: The New Economics of the MinimumWage (Princeton, N.J.: Princeton University Press, 1997); and David Neumark and William L. Wascher, Minimum Wages (Cambridge, Mass.: MIT Press, 2010).

[40] See Government Accountability Office, Multiple Employment and Training Programs: Providing Information on Colocating Services and Consolidating Administrative Structures Could Promote Efficiencies, GAO-11-92 (February 9, 2011), www.gao.gov/products/ GAO-11-92. GAO estimates that the federal government spent about $12 billion on training programs in fiscal year 2010.

[41] See Organisation for Economic Co-operation and Development, OECD Employment Outlook: 2011 (Paris: OECD, September 2011), pp. 264–273, www.oecd.org/ employ ment/outlook.

[42] For example, the United States spent $30 billion on Pell grants during the 2009–2010 academic year. About $12 billion of that total was spent on independent students attending two-year or proprietary institutions. See Department of Education, Office of Postsecondary Education, 2009–2010 Federal Pell Grant Program End-of-Year Report (undated), www2.ed.gov/finaid/prof/ resources/data/pell-2009-10/pell-eoy-2009-10.html.

[43] For reviews, see David Card, Jochen Kluve, and Andrea Weber, "Active Labor Market Policy Evaluations: A Meta-Analysis," Economic Journal, vol. 120, no. 548 (November 2010), pp. F452– F477; and James J. Heckman, Robert J. LaLonde, and Jeffrey A. Smith, "The Economics and Econometrics of Active Labor Market Programs," in Orley Ashenfelter and David Card, eds., Handbook of Labor Economics (Amsterdam: Elsevier B.V./North Holland, 1999), pp. 1865–2097.

[44] General Accounting Office (now the Government Accountability Office), Job Training Partnership Act: Long-term Earnings and Employment Outcomes, GAO/HEHS-96-40 (March 1996); and Peter R. Mueser, Kenneth R. Troske, and Alexey Gorislavsky, "Using State Administrative Data to Measure Program Performance," Review of Economics and Statistics, vol. 89, no. 4 (November 2007), pp. 761–783.

[45] Louis Jacobson, Robert LaLonde, and Daniel Sullivan. "Estimating the Returns to Community College Schooling for Displaced Workers," Journal of Econometrics, vol. 125, nos. 1-2 (2005), pp. 271–304.

[46] For a review of successful sectoral training programs, see Sheila Maguire and others, Tuning In to Local Labor Markets: Findings from the Sectoral Employment Impact Study (Public/Private Ventures, July 2010), www.ppv.org/ppv/publication.asp?sectionjd=26&searchjd=&publicationjd=325.

[47] See James J. Kemple, Career Academies: Impacts on Labor Market Outcomes and Educational Attainment (New York: MDRC, March 2004), www.mdrc. org/publications/366/overview.html.

[48] See Megan Millenky and others, Staying on Course: Three Year Results of the National Guard Youth ChallenNGe Evaluation (New York: MDRC, June 2011), www.mdrc.org/publications/ 599/overview.html.

[49] See Robert I. Lerman, Lauren Eyster, and Kate Chambers, The Benefits and Challenges of Registered Apprenticeship: The Sponsors' Perspective (report submitted by the Urban Institute to the Department of Labor, March 2009), www.urban.org/ publications/411907.html; and Pahl Gunn and Lalith De Silva, Registered Apprenticeship: Findings from Site Visits to Five States (report submitted by Planmatics to the Department of Labor, November 2008), http://wdr.doleta.gov/research/keyword .cfm?fuseaction=dsp_resultDetails&pub_id=2404&mp=y.

[50] See Kevin Hollenbeck, "State Use of Workforce System Net Impact Estimates and Rates of Return" (paper presented at the Association for Public Policy Analysis and Management Conference, Los Angeles, November 7, 2008), http://research .upjohn.org/confpapers/1.

[51] See Anne Roder and Mark Elliott, A Promising Start: Year Up's Initial Impacts on Low-Income Young Adults' Careers (New York: Economic Mobility Corporation, April 2011), www.economic mobilitycorp.org.

[52] See Bruce D. Meyer, "Lessons from the U.S. Unemployment Insurance Experiments," Journal of Economic Literature, vol. 33, no. 1 (March 1995), pp. 91–131.

[53] Other population subgroups such as unemployed single parents also participated in the ERA demonstration. The only group that experienced sustained positive benefits was the long-term unemployed. See Richard Hendra and others, Breaking the Low-Pay, No-Pay Cycle: Final Evidence from the U.K. Employment Retention and Advancement (ERA) Demonstration, Research Report 765 (United Kingdom Department for Work and Pensions, August 2011), http://research.dwp.gov.uk/asd/asd5/report_abstracts/ rr_abstracts/rra_ 765.asp.

[54] See Gretchen Kirby and others, Responses to Personal Reemployment Accounts (PRAs): Findings from the Demonstration States (report submitted by Mathematica Policy Research, Inc., to the Department of Labor, June 2008), www.mathematica-mpr.com/labor/ pra.asp.

[55] See Jeffrey Salzman and others, Evaluation of the Career Advancement Accounts Demonstration Project: An Implementation Study (report submitted by Social Policy Research Associates to the Department of Labor, November 2010), http://wdr.doleta.gov/research/FullText_Documents/ETAOP_2011-17.pdf.

[56] See Sheena McConnell and others, Managing Customers' Training Choices: Findings from the Individual Training Account Experiment (report submitted by Mathematica Policy Research, Inc., to the Department of Labor, December 2006), www.mathematica-mpr.com/labor/ita.asp.

[57] See Howard S. Bloom and others, "Testing a Financial Incentive to Promote Re-employment Among Displaced Workers: The Canadian Earnings Supplement Program (ESP)," Journal of Policy Analysis and Management, vol. 20, no. 3 (Summer 2001), pp. 505–523.

[58] See Pierre Cahuc and Stephane Carcillo, "Is Short-Time Work a Good Method to Keep Unemployment Down?" Nordic Economic Policy Review, vol. 1, pp. 133–164, www.norden.org/en/ publications/publikationer/2011-544.

[59] See Alison M. Shelton, Compensated Work Sharing Arrangements (Short-Time Compensation) as an Alternative to Layoffs, CRS Report for Congress R40689 (Congressional Research Service, January 4, 2012); and Wayne Vroman and Vera Brusentsev, "Short-Time Compensation as a Policy to Stabilize Employment" (Washington, D.C.: Urban Institute, November 2009), www.urban.org/publications/411983.html.

[60] For discussion of those wage losses, see Congressional Budget Office, Losing a Job During a Recession.

[61] See Dan A. Black, Jose C. Galdo, and Jeffrey A. Smith, "Evaluating the Worker Profiling and Reemployment Services System Using a Regression Discontinuity Approach," American Economic Review, vol. 97, no. 2 (May 2007), pp.104–107; and Paul T. Decker and others, Assisting Unemployment Insurance Claimants: The Long-Term Impacts of the Job Search Assistance Demonstration (report submitted by Mathematica Policy Research, Inc., to the Department of Labor, February 2000), www.upjohninst.org/erdc/ auic.html.

[62] See Christopher J. O'Leary, "State UI Job Search Rules and Reemployment Services," Monthly Labor Review, vol. 129, no. 6 (June 2006), pp. 27–37, www.bls.gov/opub/mlr/ 2006/06/art3abs.htm.

[63] Meyer, "Lessons from the U.S. Unemployment Insurance Experiments"; and Louis S. Jacobson, "Strengthening One-Stop Career Centers: Helping More Unemployed Workers Find Jobs and Build Skills," Brookings Hamilton Project Discussion Paper 2009-01 (April 2009), www.brookings.edu/papers/2009/ 0402_jobs_skills_jacobson.aspx.

[64] Many states and localities offer some form of skill or work readiness certification. Those programs are generally aimed at less-skilled workers and may require some form of training before clients can take certification exams. Examples include the Workforce Alliance for Growth in the Economy (WAGE) certificate program, which is conducted by the Arkansas Department of Career Education, and the Workforce Skills Certification System, which was developed by Comprehensive Adult Student Assessment Systems and is used in California, Connecticut, Oregon, and Washington. See Norma Rey-Alicea and Geri Scott, A Survey of Selected Work Readiness Certificates (prepared by Jobs for the Future for Skill Up Rhode Island, January 2007), www.jff.org/publications/ workforce/survey-selected-work-readiness-certifica/364.

In: High Unemployment: Select Analyses
Editors: L. Sandidge and V. Irby
ISBN: 978-1-62257-994-5

Chapter 2

UNEMPLOYMENT INSURANCE ECONOMIC CIRCUMSTANCES OF INDIVIDUALS WHO EXHAUSTED BENEFITS*

United States Government Accountability Office

ABBREVIATIONS

ASEC	Annual Social and Economic Supplement
CPS	Current Population Survey
HHS	Department of Health and Human Services
Labor	Department of Labor
Recovery Act	American Recovery and Reinvestment Act of 2009
SNAP	Supplemental Nutrition Assistance Program
TANF	Temporary Assistance for Needy Families
UI	Unemployment Insurance
USDA	Department of Agriculture

* This is an edited, reformatted and augmented version of United States Government Accountability Office publication, Report to the Chairman, Committee on Finance, U.S. Senate, Report GAO-12-408, dated February 2012.

Why GAO Did This Study

The recession of 2007 to 2009 was the most severe in the United States since the 1930s, resulting in a net loss of 7.5 million jobs. Workers who lose a job through no fault of their own (referred to as "displaced workers" in this chapter) may turn to financial assistance offered through the Unemployment Insurance (UI) program. Currently, through benefit extensions authorized by Congress, eligible displaced workers can receive UI benefits for up to 99 weeks in certain states. However, with the slow economic recovery, some may exhaust UI benefits without finding a new job. This raises questions about how Temporary Assistance for Needy Families (TANF), a program that provides cash assistance to low-income families with children, and other support programs are aiding those who have exhausted UI benefits.

GAO was asked to examine: (1) how many of the workers who lost jobs in the recession received and exhausted UI; (2) what are the economic circumstances of those who exhausted UI, and how many received support from TANF and other programs; and (3) the extent to which UI agencies refer those exhausting UI to other support programs. GAO analyzed data from the Current Population Survey's 2008 and 2010 Displaced Worker Supplements and the 2010 Annual Social and Economic Supplement and data from the Departments of Labor and Health and Human Services. GAO also surveyed 51 state UI agencies and conducted interviews with 16 state TANF agencies, selected to reflect a range of unemployment rate changes in recent years.

GAO is making no recommendations in this chapter.

What GAO Found

Among the 15 million workers who lost jobs from 2007 to 2009, half received Unemployment Insurance (UI), and about one-fourth of the recipients exhausted UI benefits by January 2010. This represents 2 million displaced workers who exhausted UI as of early 2010, the most recent survey data available. Labor estimated that about an additional 3-1/2 million individuals exhausted benefits in 2010 and 2011.

Many of the displaced workers who exhausted UI by January 2010 appear to have faced difficult economic circumstances. Their unemployment rate was high—46 percent in January 2010. Most, however, appeared to have worked at some point in 2009 or to have been supported by another household member who was working, and some had income from assets, such as interest or dividends.

Nevertheless, the poverty rate of displaced workers who exhausted UI was higher than the rate among working-age adults—18 percent compared to 13 percent, and more than 40 percent had relatively low incomes, below 200 percent of the federal poverty threshold (see figure). Few (less than 3 percent) of the households of those who exhausted UI received TANF benefits in 2009.

Most would not have qualified for TANF because they did not have children age 18 or younger, a general TANF eligibility criteria. More of these households received benefits from Social Security programs (18 percent) and the Supplemental Nutrition Assistance Program (15 percent for the program formerly known as the Food Stamp Program).

While there are no federal requirements to refer those exhausting UI benefits to other support programs, most (45) of the state UI agencies GAO surveyed reported providing such individuals with information or connecting them to support programs.

UI agencies made these connections in a variety of ways, such as through websites, mail, staff referrals, and interagency coordination.

For example, Washington state has a multiagency workgroup which developed a resource guide that was mailed to those exhausting UI benefits and posted online and established a phone number to handle questions from these individuals.

Income-to-Poverty Ratios of Individuals Who Exhausted UI Compared to Civilian Working-Age Adults, Based on Annual Family Incomes in 2009

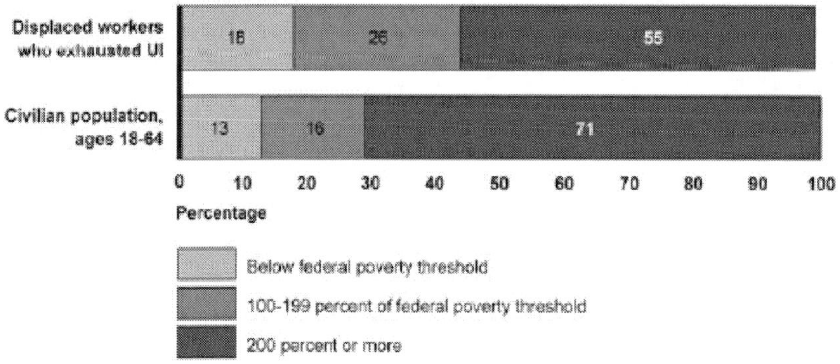

Source: GAO Aanalysis of Current Population Survey.Displaced Worker Supplement and Annual Social and Economic Supplement, 2010.

Note: Percentages may not total 100 due to rounding.

February 17, 2012

The Honorable Max Baucus
Chairman
Committee on Finance United States Senate

Dear Mr. Chairman:

The recession from 2007 to 2009 was the most severe in the United States since the Great Depression of the 1930s. From the start of the recession in December 2007 to its official end in June 2009, the U.S. lost a net total of 7.5 million jobs. Since then, the economy has been slow to recover. In January 2012, the unemployment rate was 8.3 percent, with more than 40 percent of the 12.8 million unemployed out of work for 6 months or longer. Workers who involuntarily lose a job—referred to as "displaced workers" in this chapter—may turn to financial assistance offered through the Unemployment Insurance (UI) program.[1] UI is a $156 billion federal-state program that temporarily and partially replaces the lost earnings of those who become unemployed through no fault of their own.[2] Typically, states provide UI benefits for up to 26 weeks. Since mid-2008, Congress and the states have temporarily extended the period of time that displaced workers can receive UI benefits to up to 99 weeks, though the maximum number of weeks of available benefits varies among the states.

However, despite the UI benefit extensions, the slow economic recovery may result in some displaced workers exhausting UI benefits without finding a new job. This raises questions about how the Temporary Assistance for Needy Families (TANF) program, one of the nation's primary income support programs for low-income families, is aiding UI exhaustees. TANF is a $16.5 billion federal block grant program that provides cash assistance and other services to low-income families with children.

You asked us to provide information about displaced workers' receipt and exhaustion of UI. In response to your request, we answered the following questions: (1) Among workers who lost jobs during the recession, how many received and exhausted UI benefits? (2) What are the economic circumstances of those who exhausted UI, and how many received assistance from TANF and other support programs? (3) To what extent do state UI agencies refer exhaustees to support programs?

To address these questions we used several different research methods. To identify the number of displaced workers who received and exhausted UI, referred to as "exhaustees" in this chapter, we analyzed data from the 2010 Displaced Worker Supplement to the January 2010 Current Population Survey (CPS) conducted by the Census Bureau, which surveyed individuals who lost jobs from 2007 to 2009.[3] We also compared some results from the 2010 Displaced Worker Supplement to data from the 2008 supplement, which surveyed individuals who lost jobs prior to the recession, from 2005 to 2007. Using data from the Displaced Worker Supplements allowed us to examine the experiences of a cohort of workers who lost jobs in the recession years and compare them to workers who lost jobs before the recession, but our results are as of January 2010 when the 2010 Displaced Worker Supplement was conducted.

To examine UI exhaustees' economic circumstances and determine how many exhaustees received supports from TANF and other federal income support programs, we analyzed data from the 2010 Displaced Worker Supplement, merged with data from the Annual Social and Economic Supplement of the 2010 CPS.[4]

Merging these two data sets allowed us to identify UI exhaustees as of January 2010 (using data from the Displaced Worker Supplement) and examine their household incomes in 2009 (using data from the Annual Social and Economic Supplement).

We also interviewed officials from 16 state TANF agencies, selected to reflect a range of changes in unemployment rates in recent years, and we analyzed data on the UI and TANF programs from the Department of Labor (Labor) and the Department of Health and Human Services (HHS). To determine the extent to which UI agencies refer exhaustees to other programs, we conducted a web-based survey with UI agencies in 50 states and the District of Columbia, obtaining responses from all 51.[5]

For all research questions, we spoke with officials at Labor who oversee the UI program and officials at HHS who oversee TANF. We also reviewed applicable federal laws and regulations, studies, and policy documents. We conducted this performance audit from March 2011 to February 2012, in accordance with generally accepted government auditing standards. Those standards require that we plan and perform the audit to obtain sufficient, appropriate evidence to provide a reasonable basis for our findings and conclusions based on our audit objectives. We believe that the evidence obtained provides a reasonable basis for our findings and conclusions based on our audit objectives (see appendix I for further information on our scope and methodology).

BACKGROUND

Unemployment Insurance Program

The UI program, established under Title III of the Social Security Act in 1935, was intended to, among other things, help those who become unemployed through no fault of their own, and help stabilize the economy during recessions. The program is generally financed by federal and state payroll taxes levied on employers. Within the guidelines of federal law, states administer the program and can specify who is eligible to receive UI benefits and how much they receive. Nationwide, UI benefit payments replaced 46 percent of a worker's previous wages in 2010 on average.[6] Applicants must have earned at least a certain amount in wages and/or have worked a certain number of weeks over a period of time to be eligible for benefits.[7] In addition, they must be available for and able to work. For their part, UI agencies must identify recipients who are likely to exhaust their benefits and refer them to re-employment services, such as those available through state run-employment centers, known as "one-stops." At these one-stops, states and localities are required to provide services for many federally funded employment and training programs, and they have the option of including additional programs, such as TANF.

Typically, eligible unemployed workers can receive UI benefits for up to 26 weeks in most states, though individuals may be eligible for fewer weeks.[8] During periods of high unemployment, states may provide up to 13 or 20 additional weeks of benefits through the Extended Benefits program, funded jointly by states and the federal government. In 2009, Congress temporarily authorized full federal financing of the Extended Benefits program[9] and later extended the authorization several times, most recently in 2011.[10] In 2008, Congress made additional weeks of benefits available through the Emergency Unemployment Compensation program, which are federally funded.[11] The Emergency Unemployment Compensation program has four tiers of benefits, the first two of which are available in all states and enable eligible UI recipients to obtain benefits for up to an additional 34 weeks. The second two tiers are only available in states with high unemployment and provide up to 19 weeks of additional benefits. In states that provide at most 26 weeks of regular UI benefits, that offer the maximum 20 weeks of Extended Benefits payments, and that are on all four tiers of Emergency Unemployment Compensation, some eligible unemployed workers may receive up to 99 weeks of UI benefits (see fig. 1). As of January 8, 2012, eligible unemployed workers could potentially receive the maximum 99 weeks of benefits in 17 states, according to Labor's data, though some individuals may be eligible for fewer weeks in these states. The Emergency Unemployment Compensation program and full federal financing of the Extended Benefits program are scheduled to expire in March 2012.

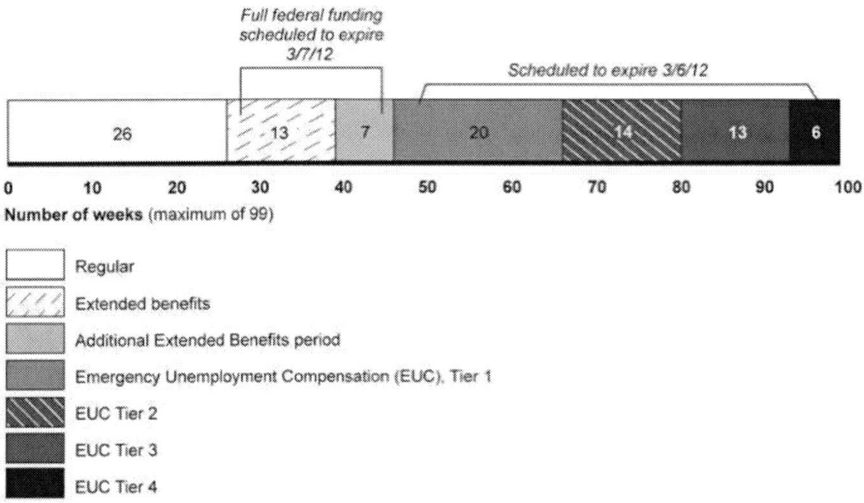

Sourc: GAO analysis of Labor documents.

Notes: The actual duration varies by state and by individual, based on how they meet states' eligibility criteria. As of January 8, 2012, eligible unemployed workers could potentially receive the maximum 99 weeks of benefits in 17 states, based on Labor's data.

Figure 1. Typical Potential Maximum Duration of UI Benefits, as of January 2012.

TANF Block Grant

The Personal Responsibility and Work Opportunity Reconciliation Act of 1996 created the TANF block grant, a $16.5 billion fixed federal funding stream allocated to states to provide a wide range of services to low-income families who have children.[12] States must maintain a specified level of spending, referred to as maintenance of effort, to get their federal TANF funds. The most recent data available show that in fiscal year 2010, states spent approximately $35.8 billion in federal and state TANF funds, with 70 percent used for programs and services other than ongoing cash assistance. As established in federal law, the goals of the TANF program are to provide assistance to needy families so that children may be cared for in their own homes or in the homes of relatives, end needy families' dependence on government benefits, reduce out-of-wedlock pregnancies, and encourage two-parent families. In line with these goals, TANF funds may be used in a variety of ways, including monthly cash assistance to low-income families, child care, employment and training, subsidized employment, transportation, and single or short-term payments for onetime urgent needs, such as for rent or utilities. States have flexibility to set eligibility requirements for TANF benefits and services and to determine the type of assistance they provide. However, federal law requires states to involve at least a specified percentage of TANF cash assistance recipients in work activities, such as participating in job training or subsidized employment. [13] States face financial penalties if they do not meet these specified rates.[14] Additionally, certain individuals who do not cooperate in establishing or enforcing child support orders face reduced levels of TANF assistance, and possible denial of all TANF benefits. In the period of the recession, states were able to draw upon two additional TANF-related funding sources. The Personal Responsibility and Work Opportunity Reconciliation Act of 1996 had created a TANF Contingency Fund of up to $2 billion that states could access in times of economic distress. Only a portion of this fund had been drawn down by the states at the start of the recession, but the fund was depleted by the end of 2009. Congress has appropriated up to $612 million for the Contingency Fund for fiscal year 2012. In 2009, Congress also created a $5 billion TANF Emergency Contingency Fund in the American Recovery and Reinvestment Act of 2009 (Recovery Act), which was made available to states that had certain increases either in their cash assistance caseloads or in their expenditures for nonrecurrent short-term benefits or subsidized employment. [15]

2 Million of Those Who Lost Jobs in the Recession Years Exhausted UI Benefits by Early 2010

Half of Workers Who Lost Jobs in the Recession Years Received UI, an Increase from Prior Years

The number of displaced workers increased substantially during the recession years, and proportionately more of them received UI than in the 3 years prior to the recession.

Specifically, from 2007 to 2009, 49 percent of the 15.4 million people who lost jobs received UI. In contrast, 36 percent of the 8.3 million people who lost jobs from 2005 to 2007 received UI (see fig. 2).[16] The UI safety net expanded during a recession that affected so many workers, as it is designed to do.

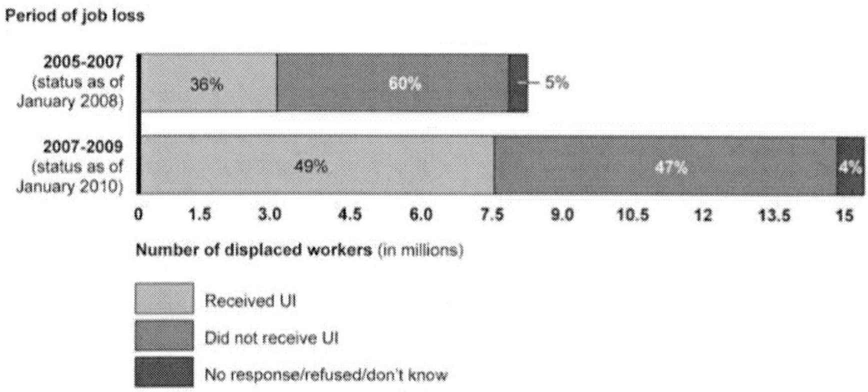

Source: GAO analysis of the Census Bureau's 2008 and 2010 Displaced Worker Supplements to the CPS.

Notes: The top bar represents data from the 2008 Displaced Worker Supplement, which was conducted in January 2008 with people ages 20 and older who experienced a job loss from 2005 to 2007. The bottom bar represents data from the 2010 Displaced Worker Supplement, which was conducted in January 2010 with people ages 20 and older who experienced a job loss from 2007 to 2009. Estimates presented in this figure have margins of error that are within plus or minus 2 percentage points. The difference in the percentages of displaced workers receiving UI between the time periods is statistically significant at the 95 percent confidence level. Percentages may not total 100 due to rounding.

Figure 2. UI Receipt among Displaced Workers.

One reason for the higher rate of UI receipt during the recession is that fewer displaced workers became re-employed quickly.

Displaced workers have diverse labor market experiences following a job loss, with some finding new work soon afterwards, while others take longer to become reemployed.

For workers displaced during the recession years, however, comparatively fewer of them found new jobs quickly.Prior to the recession, 30 percent of displaced workers did not receive UI and were working again within 5 weeks of losing their job, compared to 18 percent of workers who lost jobs in the recession years.

Lower-Wage Workers Were Less Likely to Receive UI

In both recessionary and nonrecessionary times, not all people who lose jobs receive UI, an issue of interest to policymakers for many years. Our previous work found that lower-wage workers were less likely to receive UI than higher-wage workers in the 1990s and early 2000s.[17] This trend continued in the recent recession. Among workers who lost jobs from 2007 to 2009, those in the bottom 30 percent in earnings were half as likely to receive UI benefits as displaced workers in the top 70 percent. However, both groups received UI at a higher rate during the recession than in the period before the recession (see fig. 3). We and others previously identified several possible reasons for the historically lower rate of UI receipt among lower-wage workers. For example, they are less likely to have met the minimum earnings required for UI eligibility, particularly if their work was intermittent or part-time. Family crises can also cause some in marginal financial situations to quit a job (for example, to care for a sick child), potentially making them ineligible for UI.[18]In the Recovery Act, Congress provided for incentive payments for states that have certain UI laws in place,[19] and low-wage workers may benefit from such laws. As of September 2011, 39 states have been approved for Recovery Act incentive payments totaling $4.4 billion (see table 1). Labor has contracted with a research organization to examine the effects of these incentive payments. The final evaluation report is due in 2013. Most of the states that did not apply for incentive payments (8 states out of 13) reported in our survey that they did not apply because of concerns about costs, such as increased benefit payments or effects on state trust funds or employers.[20] Additionally, in our survey, 11 states responded that their state had enacted laws resulting in more stringent eligibility requirements or decreased coverage, such as reducing the maximum number of weeks UI benefits could be provided or increasing the wage level needed to qualify for UI.

2 Million Displaced Workers Exhausted UI by January 2010, with More since Then

Two million of the 7.5 million workers who lost jobs from 2007 to 2009 and received UI had exhausted their UI benefits by January 2010, based on the 2010 Displaced Worker Supplement (see fig. 4).[21]

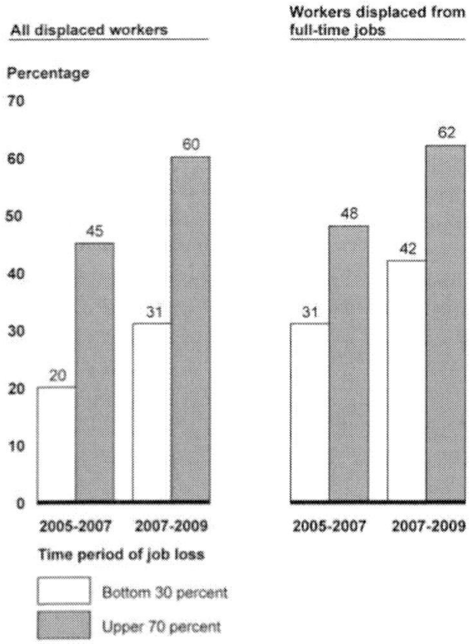

Source: GAO analysis of the 2008 and 2010 Disolaced Worker Supplements to the CPS.

Notes: This figure represents data on all displaced workers with information on average weekly wages. Estimates presented in the figure have margins of error that are within plus or minus 4 percentage points. Differences in UI receipt between displaced workers in the bottom 30 percent and top 70 percent in average weekly wages are statistically significant at the 95 percent confidence level in all four comparisons presented above. In this analysis, among all displaced workers, those in the bottom 30 percent had wages of $380 per week or less in the 2005-2007 time frame and wages of $418 per week or less in the 2007-2009 time frame. We also conducted the analysis using the same cut-off points ($380, adjusting for inflation) for defining the lower-wage group in both time periods and obtained similar results. See appendix I for further information.

Figure 3. Percentage of Displaced Workers Receiving UI, Comparing Workers in the Bottom 30 Percent and Top 70 Percent in Average Weekly Earnings.

While this number is based on the most recent data available, it does not include those who may have exhausted their benefits after the survey was conducted.[22] Nevertheless, the 2007 to 2009 period numbers about 700,000 more who exhausted benefits than in the earlier period.

Also, a smaller percentage of those displaced in the 2007 to 2009 period exhausted UI (27 percent) than in the earlier period (44 percent), likely reflecting to some extent the availability of additional weeks of UI benefits (see fig. 5).

Table 1. Number of States Receiving Recovery Act Incentive Funds

	States that received funds for an existing law[a]	States that received funds for changing law or regulation	Total number of states
States must have in place the following to receive one-third of their incentive payment[b]			
A base period that includes recent wages	19	20	39
States must have in place at least two of the following four to receive two-thirds of their incentive payments[c]			
No denial of benefits for seeking part-time work	8	18	26
No disqualification for separations from employment for compelling family reasons	1	18	19
Provide extended compensation to UI recipients in qualifying training programs	0	16	16
Provide dependents' allowances to UI recipients with dependents	4	3	7
Number of states that have been approved for 1/3 of their payment			39
Number of states that have been approved for all of their payments			34

Note: Puerto Rico and the Virgin Islands, which both received Recovery Act incentive funds, are not included in this table.

[a] Incentive funds were also provided to states that already had the specific policies in place. This also includes states that clarified procedures to ensure that current law is interpreted in a way that meets the requirements for approval.

[b] To obtain the first one-third of incentive payments, the state must generally use a base period that includes the most recent quarter before the start of the benefit year. The base period is the time period during which wages earned or hours/weeks worked are examined to determine a worker's monetary entitlement to UI.

[c] States that qualify for the first one-third can obtain the remaining two-thirds if their state meets 2 of the following 4 requirements: (1) the state generally cannot deny UI payments to an individual solely because that person is seeking only part-time work, (2) the state shall not disqualify a person from receiving UI payments for separating from employment if that separation is for a compelling family reason, (3) UI payments must generally be available for individuals who have exhausted their regular UI payment and are making progress in certain training programs, and (4) the state must generally provide dependents' allowances to individuals entitled to regular UI payments and who have any dependents.

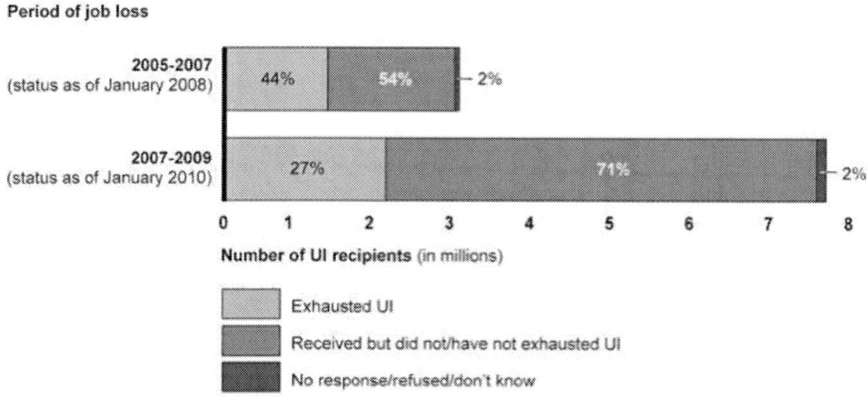

Source: GAO analysis of data from the 2008 and 2010 Displaced Worker Supplements to the CPS.

Notes: Estimates presented in this figure have margins of error that are within plus or minus 3 percentage points. The difference in the exhaustion rate between the two time periods is statistically significant at the 95 percent confidence level.

Figure 4. Benefit Exhaustion among Displaced Workers Who Received UI.

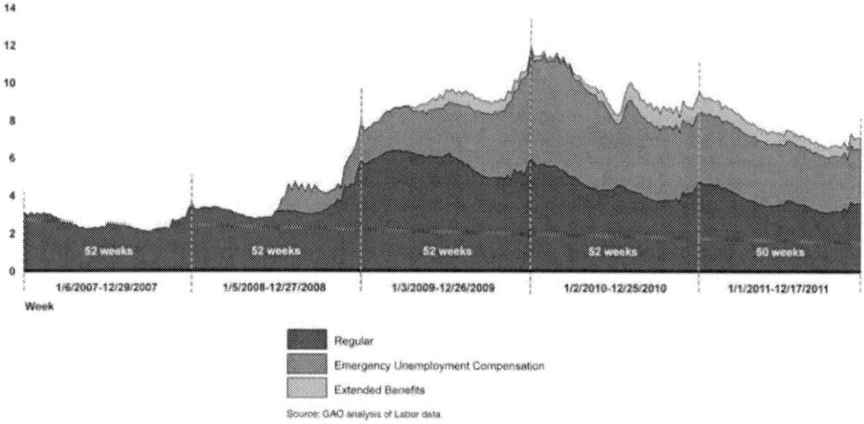

Source: GAO analysis of Labor data.

Notes: A small number (about 2 percent) of UI claimants received UI benefits from other programs, including those for federal government employees, ex-service members, individuals affected by disasters, participants in the Trade Adjustment Assistance program, and individuals receiving UI benefits for reduced work hours. Claimants in these programs are not shown in the figure above.

Figure 5. Weekly UI Claims, by UI Program.

Other data show that significant numbers of people have continued to receive and exhaust UI benefits in 2010 and 2011. For example, the number of people claiming the benefit extensions from the Emergency Unemployment Compensation and Extended Benefits programs continued to be substantial in both these years, beyond the official end of the recession in June 2009 (see fig. 5). In addition, Labor's Employment and Training Administration, which oversees state unemployment programs, provided us with estimates that there were 1.6 million exhaustees in calendar year 2010 and 2.0 million in 2011.[23]

The relatively large numbers of UI exhaustees and UI beneficiaries must be seen in the context of the extremely poor labor market conditions in recent years, when job seekers have faced bleak job prospects. Data from the Bureau of Labor Statistics show that the number of unemployed persons per job opening increased from 1.8 when the recession began in December 2007 to 6.1 when the recession officially ended in June 2009 (see figure 6). This ratio has declined to 4.2 unemployed persons per job opening in November 2011, the most recent data available, remaining above prerecession levels.

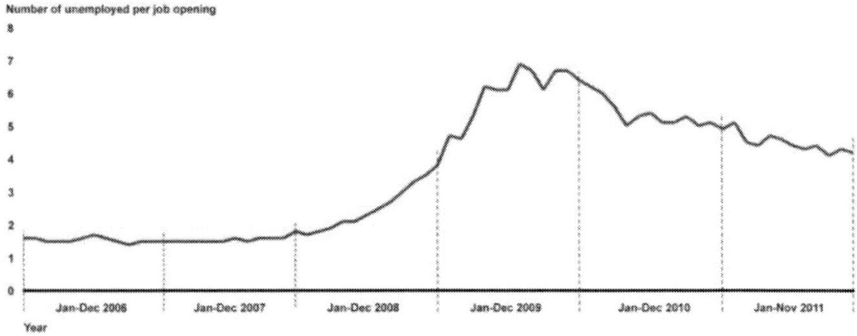

Source: Bureau of Labor Statistics.

Figure 6. Unemployed Persons per Job Opening.

Many UI Exhaustees Faced Difficult Economic Circumstances, but Few Were Likely to Qualify for TANF

18 Percent of Exhaustees Were in Poverty in 2009

For those who lost jobs from 2007 to 2009 and exhausted UI, the CPS data suggest that many faced difficult economic circumstances. Many were still not employed in January 2010 and those with employment often had reduced earnings. It is unknown whether the situations of these exhaustees have improved or worsened since then because more current data are not available.

More specifically, an estimated 46 percent of UI exhaustees who lost jobs in the recession years were unemployed at the time they were surveyed in January 2010 (see fig. 7). About a third (35 percent) of the exhaustees were re-employed in January, a smaller proportion than in the period before the recession (57 percent).

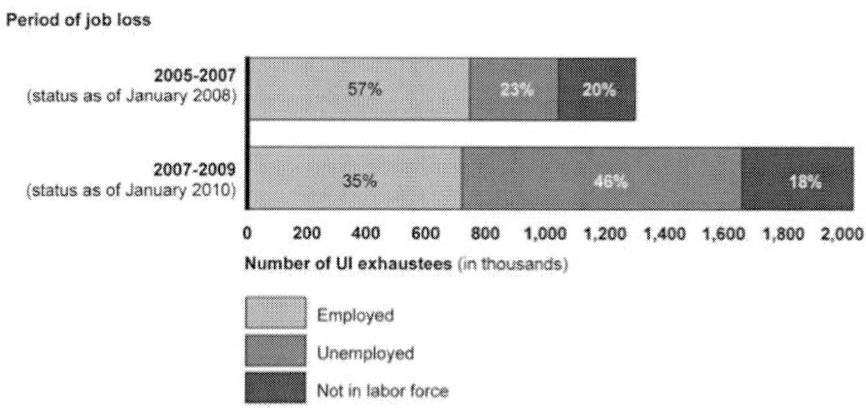

Source: GAO analysis of data from the 2008 and 2010 Displaced Worker Supplements to the CPS.

Notes: Estimates presented in this figure have margins of error within plus or minus 5 percentage points. Differences in the percentages of exhaustees who were employed and unemployed between the two time frames are statistically significant at the 95 percent confidence level. Percentages may not total 100 due to rounding.

Figure 7. Employment Status of Displaced Workers Who Exhausted UI.

Among the exhaustees who were unemployed in January 2010, about half appeared to have worked at some point in the previous year. An estimated 50 percent had some earnings in 2009.

These workers might have done temporary work at some point in 2009, worked in a short-term or a seasonal job, or found a new job but then were laid-off again.

Among those UI exhaustees who lost jobs in the recession years and were re-employed, 71 percent experienced a reduction in earnings.[24]

Table 2. Percentage of UI Exhaustees' Households with Private Income Sources, 2009

Private income source	Estimated percentage of UI exhaustees with income source in 2009
UI exhaustee's own wages, salaries, or self-employment income	63%
Wages, salaries, or self-employment income from other household members	65
Any earnings, from UI exhaustee or household members	87
Interest income[a]	34
Dividends[b]	16
Retirement income[c]	<11
Rental income[d]	<9
Any income from interest, retirement, dividends, rental	43
Child support	<7
Alimony	0
Any of the above income sources in the household	91

Source: GAO analysis of the CPS, 2010 Displaced Worker Supplement merged with data from the 2010 Annual Social and Economic Supplement.

Notes: This table presents data on the income sources in 2009 of the 2 million people ages 20 and older who lost a job from 2007 to 2009, received UI, and exhausted it as of January 2010, and as such, may not reflect the circumstances of individuals directly after exhausting UI. Estimates presented in this table have margin of errors within plus or minus 5 percentage points. Point estimates are suppressed where the margin of error of the estimate exceeds 30 percent of the point estimate. For these estimates, we are reporting the upper bound of the 95 percent confidence interval. All estimates in the table are significantly different from zero, with the exception of alimony. There were no households who received alimony in the sample.

[a] Includes payments received (or have credited to accounts) from bonds, treasury notes, IRAs, certificates of deposit, interest-bearing savings and checking accounts, and all other investments that pay interest.

[b] Includes payments received from stock holdings and mutual fund shares. The CPS does not include capital gains from the sale of stock holdings as income.

[c] Includes pension or retirement income received from companies or unions, federal government (civil service), military, state or local governments, railroad retirement, annuities or paid-up insurance policies, individual retirement accounts, Keogh, or 401(k) payments, or other retirement income.

[d] Includes net income people received from the rental of a house, store, or other property, receipts from boarders or lodgers, net royalty income, and periodic payments from estate or trust funds.

The median earnings replacement ratio was 0.74, meaning that half of re-employed exhaustees experienced a reduction in earnings greater than 26 percent, while the other half experienced a reduction of less than 26 percent or an earnings increase. In addition to data on exhaustees' employment and earnings, information on household income provides a broader perspective on how exhaustees have fared. These data suggest that some exhaustees may have been helped by other sources of income, such as a household member who was earning income in 2009, or income from assets, such as interest or dividends.

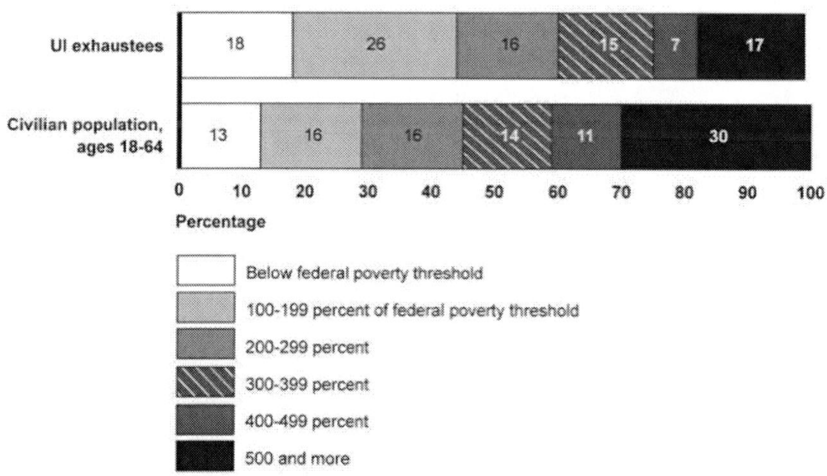

Source: Data on UI exhaustees is from GAO analysis of data from the 2010 Displaced Worker Supplement to the CPS merged with the 2010 Annual Social and Economic Supplement. Data on the civilian population is from the 2010 Annual Social and Economic Supplement.

Notes. Percentages may not total 100 percent due to rounding. The top bar on UI exhaustees presents 2009 data on the 2.0 million people, ages 20 and older, who lost jobs from 2007 to 2009, received UI, and exhausted UI by January 2010. It may not reflect the circumstances of individuals directly after exhausting UI. Estimates presented in this figure have margins of error that are within plus or minus 6 percentage points. Differences between UI exhaustees and the civilian population age 18-64 in the percentage below poverty and the percentage below 200 percent of the federal poverty threshold are statistically significant at the 95 percent confidence level.

Figure 8. Income-to-Poverty Ratios of UI Exhaustees Compared to Working-Age Civilian Adults, Based on 2009 Annual Family Incomes.

About two-thirds of exhaustees had a household member with some wage or salary earnings in 2009. About 40 percent of exhaustees' households had some income from assets, namely interest, dividends, retirement, or rental income. In total, about 90 percent of UI exhaustees had some private income sources within their household during calendar year 2009 (table 2).

Nevertheless, while the annual income levels of UI exhaustees varied in 2009, their poverty rate was higher than that of other working-age adults (ages 18 to 64).[25] Specifically, 18 percent of UI exhaustees were in poverty, in contrast to 13 percent of working-age adults (see fig. 8). Furthermore, about 40 percent of UI exhaustees had incomes under 200 percent of the federal poverty threshold, compared to about 30 percent of working-age adults.

Few UI Exhaustees Received Aid from TANF

Supplemental Nutrition Assistance Program (SNAP)

SNAP is intended to help low-income individuals and families obtain a better diet by supplementing their incomes with benefits to purchase food. SNAP is jointly administered by the U.S. Department of Agriculture (USDA) and state governments, with USDA paying the full cost of SNAP benefits and approximately half of states' administrative costs. SNAP benefits are provided to all households who apply and are found eligible. Eligibility for SNAP is based primarily on a household's income and assets. In addition, federal regulations set forth when households become automatically, or categorically, eligible for SNAP if they are already receiving certain cash or noncash benefits from certain other federal programs for low-income families, such as TANF.

According to USDA data, SNAP provided food and nutrition assistance to approximately 21 million households on average each month in fiscal year 2011, totaling almost $72 billion in benefits for the year. From fiscal year 2008 to 2011, the number of households receiving SNAP benefits has increased by approximately 66 percent, and the cost of the program has doubled. According to USDA, the downturn in the U.S. economy, coupled with changes in the program's rules and administration, has led to an increase in the number of SNAP participants. While SNAP participation increases drove subsequent cost increases, the 2009 Recovery Act also impacted SNAP costs by providing a temporary across-the-board increase to the SNAP benefit amount.

Table 3. Receipt of Benefits from Government Programs within UI Exhaustee Households, 2009

Support programs	Estimated percentage receiving benefit
Social Security retirement, Disability Insurance, or survivors	18%
SNAP	15
Supplemental Security Income	<6
Disability benefits, other than Social Security[a]	<4
TANF or other welfare[b]	<3
Workers' compensation	<3
Veterans benefits	<2
Any of the above government programs[c]	34

Source: GAO analysis of the CPS, 2010 Displaced Worker Supplement, merged with data from the 2010 Annual Social and Economic Supplement.

Notes: This table presents data on government benefits received in 2009 by any household member of a UI exhaustee (the 2.0 million people ages 20 and older who lost a job from 2007 to 2009, received UI, and exhausted it as of January 2010). For example, a household would be counted as receiving Social Security benefits if the spouse of a UI exhaustee received Social Security benefits and not the exhaustee himself. The data shown includes all exhaustees, regardless of whether they were employed, unemployed, or not in the labor force at the time of the January 2010 survey. The data may not reflect the circumstances of individuals directly after exhausting UI. Point estimates are suppressed where the margin of error of the estimate exceeds 30 percent of the point estimate. For these estimates, we are reporting the upper bound of the 95 percent confidence interval. All estimates in the table are significantly different from zero. For point estimates that we present in the table, the 95 percent confidence intervals are: 14 to 22 percent for Social Security retirement, Disability Insurance, or survivors benefits; 11 to 18 percent for SNAP; and 29 to 39 percent for receipt of any of the government programs we included in our analysis.

[a] Includes disability benefits provided by workers' compensation, companies or unions, federal government (civil service), military, state or local governments, railroad retirement, accident or disability insurance, Black lung payments, state temporary sickness, or other disability payments.

[b] Includes any cash assistance, even for one month, from a state or county welfare program including welfare or welfare-to-work programs, TANF, Aid to Families with Dependent Children (the name of the federal welfare program that was replaced by TANF in 1996), General Assistance/Emergency Assistance program, Diversion Payments, Refugee Cash and Medical Assistance program, General Assistance from Bureau of Indian Affairs, or Tribal Administered General Assistance.

[c] Includes programs listed in the table, as well as survivors benefits other than Social Security (from pensions, estates, trusts, or annuities, private companies or unions; federal government (civil service), military, state or local governments, railroad retirement, workers' compensation, Black lung payments, and other survivor payments). The sample size for survivors benefits other than Social Security was too small to present the estimate.

In 2009, few UI exhaustees were likely to have received TANF support, which is targeted to very low-income families with children. The majority of UI exhaustees would not have qualified because they did not have a minor child—55 percent of exhaustees did not have a child age 18 or younger in their household.[26] Among the 18 percent of exhaustees in poverty, less than half (48 percent) had minor children. Overall, only 9 percent of exhaustees had a child age 18 or under, as well as income below the federal poverty threshold, two general criteria for TANF eligibility though the specific criteria vary by state.[27]

Data derived from the CPS show that less than 3 percent of UI exhaustees' households received financial assistance from TANF or other welfare programs in 2009 (see table 3).[28] Overall, about one-third of exhaustees' households received at least one government support in that year. Significantly more of the households of UI exhaustees received benefits from Social Security programs (18 percent for retirement, Disability Insurance, and survivors programs) or Supplemental Nutrition Assistance Program (SNAP, formerly known as the Food Stamp Program)(15 percent) than from TANF.

With regard to Social Security, 21 percent of UI exhaustees' households received benefits from the retirement, Disability Insurance, survivors, or Supplemental Security Income programs.[29] Other than Supplemental Security Income, the CPS data do not distinguish among the types of Social Security benefits a household received, but 7 percent of exhaustees were age 62 or older in January 2010 and therefore potentially eligible for Social Security retirement benefits (see fig. 9).[30] Some exhaustees may have received the other types of Social Security benefits, or they may have been residing with a household member who received Social Security benefits.

The estimated percentage of exhaustee households receiving TANF may be slightly higher among those households more closely aligned with the TANF target population.

Among the households of UI exhaustees that had minor children and income below 200 percent of the federal poverty threshold, less than 10 percent received TANF or other welfare benefits in 2009 (see table 4).[31] More than one-third of these households received SNAP benefits.

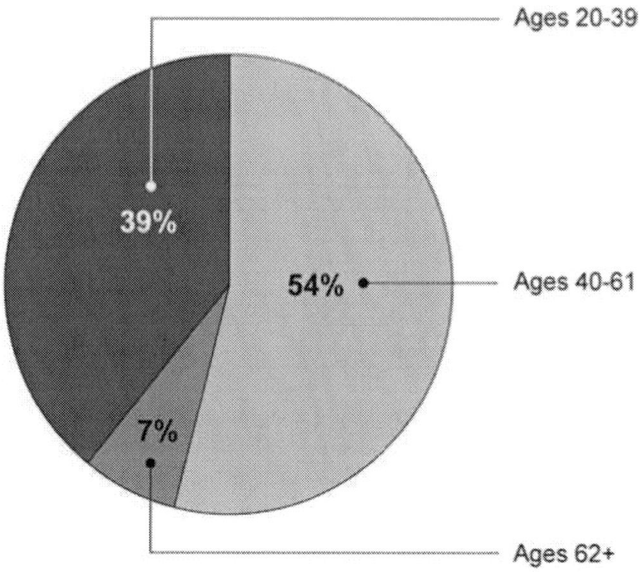

Source: GAO analysis of the 2010 Displaced Worker Supplement to the CPS.

Notes: This figure presents the ages in January 2010 of the 2.0 million people ages 20 and over who lost a job from 2007 to 2009, received UI, and exhausted it as of January 2010. Estimates presented in this figure have margins of error that are within plus or minus 4 percentage points.

Figure 9. Ages of UI Exhaustees, January 2010.

Regarding the use of TANF benefits by UI exhaustees or others who have lost jobs, state TANF officials we spoke with offered several reasons why they may not have sought or received such assistance. One official noted that some may not have sought TANF because they may still have some resources or assets that they can rely on. Such assets may also make a person ineligible for TANF since nearly all states consider the value of a family's assets when determining their eligibility for ongoing TANF cash assistance.[32] Other state officials said that some workers who recently lost jobs may be reluctant to seek TANF due to its work activity or child support requirements, particularly given the fact that the TANF benefit is low.[33] Some officials also noted that the restrictions on work activities that limit the amount of time that can be spent on education and training may not match the needs of displaced workers, who may require more education or retraining to find a new job.[34] Finally, several state officials told us that some people who recently lost jobs may not apply for TANF because they perceive a stigma attached to being a welfare recipient.[35]

Table 4. Receipt of Benefits from Government Programs within Households of UI Exhaustees with Minor Children and Annual Incomes Below 200 Percent of the Federal Poverty Threshold, 2009

Support programs	Estimated percentage receiving benefit
SNAP	38%
Social Security retirement, Disability Insurance, or survivors	<25
TANF or other welfare[a]	<10
Supplemental Security Income	<10
Any of the above government programs[b]	49

Source: GAO analysis of the CPS, 2010 Displaced Worker Supplement, merged with data from the 2010 Annual Social and Economic Supplement.

Notes: This table presents data on sources of household income in 2009 for the approximately 460,000 of UI exhaustees with children age 18 or under in the household and incomes below 200 percent of the federal poverty threshold. UI exhaustees are people ages 20 and older who lost a job from 2007 to 2009, received UI, and exhausted it as of January 2010. This includes exhaustees regardless of whether they were employed, unemployed, or not in the labor force at the time of the survey. The data may not reflect the circumstances of individuals directly after exhausting UI. A household is counted as receiving a government benefit if any household member received the benefit. For example, a household would be counted as receiving Social Security benefits if the spouse of a UI exhaustee received Social Security benefits and not the exhaustee himself. Point estimates are suppressed where the margin of error of the estimate exceeds 30 percent of the point estimate. For these estimates, we are reporting the upper bound of the 95 percent confidence interval. All estimates in the table are significantly different from zero. For point estimates that we present in the table, the 95 percent confidence intervals are: 28 to 49 percent for SNAP, and 38 to 60 percent for receipt of any of the government programs we included in our analysis. The confidence interval for Social Security retirement, Disability Insurance, or survivors benefits is 9 to 25 percent.

[a] Includes any cash assistance, even for one month, from a state or county welfare program including welfare or welfare-to-work programs, TANF, Aid to Families with Dependent Children (the name of the federal welfare program that was replaced by TANF in 1996), General Assistance/Emergency Assistance program, Diversion Payments, Refugee Cash and Medical Assistance program, General Assistance from Bureau of Indian Affairs, or Tribal Administered General Assistance.

[b] Includes programs listed in the table, as well as veterans' benefits, disability and survivors benefits other than Social Security, and workers' compensation. Sample sizes for these programs were too small to present individual estimates.

TANF Benefits and Services Provided Since the Recession

From fiscal years 2008 to 2011, HHS data show a 15 percent increase nationwide in the number of families who received TANF ongoing monthly cash assistance, from an average of 1.7 million families per month in fiscal year 2008 to an average of 1.9 million families per month during the first 9 months of fiscal year 2011. Caseload changes varied in the individual states, with 39 states experiencing increases in the number of families receiving ongoing TANF cash assistance and 12 experiencing caseload declines. Data are not available, however, to indicate whether there was an increase in the number of families receiving other forms of TANF assistance. The most recent data available show that in fiscal year 2010, states spent approximately $35.8 billion in federal and state TANF funds, with 70 percent used for programs and services other than ongoing cash assistance.

Interviews with TANF officials in 16 states suggest they provided a wide range of services throughout the recession, in part funded through Recovery Act funds. Many of these states reported providing families with some of the following: one-time emergency benefits for housing, winter heat assistance, child care, food (such as through food banks, vouchers, or meal programs), transportation, education, and clothing allowances. Most of these states used Recovery Act funds for subsidized employment programs.

In addition, with many states facing budget deficits related to the economic recession, several of the state officials discussed with us challenges in serving those affected by the recession. Officials we interviewed in 7 of the 16 states said that their states have decreased funding for the TANF program since the recession began. With regard to federal funds, as a block grant, the TANF allocations that states receive are not adjusted for caseload size, and the amounts have not been adjusted for inflation since 1996. Collectively, states in economic distress can access up to $612 million in the TANF Contingency Fund in fiscal year 2012, but they must spend more than a specified amount of state funds to do so. Other TANF funding sources that states had access to during the recession have expired. For example, nearly all 51 states accessed TANF Emergency Contingency Funds provided in the Recovery Act, but these funds expired at the end of fiscal year 2010. In addition, TANF supplemental funds, which had been awarded to 17 states with historically low welfare spending per person and high population growth, expired in June 2011. In our interviews, officials said that budgetary constraints have led to decreased spending on work supports, such as employment and training services and childcare, hiring freezes, and, also greater enforcement of time limits. States must restrict most families to a lifetime limit of 60 months of federally funded TANF cash assistance, but they may use state funds to continue benefits for families reaching the limit. In our interviews, some state officials said that budgetary constraints had led their states to discontinue these payments.

Most State UI Agencies Reported Efforts to Provide UI Exhaustees with Information about Other Support Programs

While there are no federal requirements to refer UI exhaustees to other support programs, most (45) of the state UI agencies we surveyed reported providing information or connections to support programs for exhaustees.[36] These connections are made in a number of ways, such as through websites, mail, staff referrals, and interagency coordination (see table 5).

States' efforts to provide information or connect exhaustees to other resources varied. For example:

- Colorado's UI website contains a list of resources for people who are exhausting benefits, including TANF and programs that provide assistance with foreclosure prevention, health insurance, and food aid.
- In Ohio, the UI agency mails letters to people who may be nearing the exhaustion of their UI benefits. The letter provides websites and phone numbers for programs that provide food assistance, cash assistance, Medicaid, and help with foreclosure prevention, child support payments, and job search.
- In Washington state, a multiagency working group created a detailed demographic analysis of potential exhaustees, shared data on exhaustees across agencies, developed a resource guide that was

mailed to exhaustees and posted online, and established a new unit of employees and a phone number to handle questions from individuals about to exhaust UI. This working group includes representatives from social and health services, veterans, commerce, higher education, and workforce agencies. These stakeholders continue to meet and share ideas regarding the coordination of outreach activities to the growing population of exhaustees, according to Washington officials.

- According to Pennsylvania officials, UI exhaustees were one of the populations Pennsylvania targeted for its subsidized employment program that was funded by TANF Recovery Act funds. Using data from the UI program, the workforce agency mailed UI exhaustees information on the subsidized employment program.

Table 5. Methods Reported by State UI Agencies to Provide Information and/or Connect UI Exhaustees with Support Programs

State UI agency responses by category	Number of states
Provides information	
Provides information on website	13
Mails information specifically to exhaustees	13
Sends emails to UI exhaustees	3
Automated phone recordings/messages provide information specifically to UI exhaustees	3
Other[a]	16
UI agency refers exhaustees	
Agency staff refer UI exhaustees to other support agencies	32
Automated technology refers UI exhaustees to other support agencies	7
Coordinates with other agencies	34
Coordinates with one-stops to provide information or connect UI exhaustees to other support programs	34
Coordinates with other support program agencies to provide information or connect UI exhaustees to other support programs	20
UI agency and other support agencies share data for purposes of facilitating enrollments of UI exhaustees in support programs	13
Agencies that do any of the above	45

Source: GAO analysis of survey data

[a] Other may include UI staff responding to specific inquiries from exhaustees and local 2-1-1 telephone numbers to connect people to services.

State UI agencies we surveyed reported limitations associated with any efforts to connect UI exhaustees with TANF, SNAP, and other support programs. State UI agencies' greatest barriers were limited UI agency resources or staff, along with a restriction on spending UI administrative funds (see fig. 10).[37]

These funds are provided by the federal government and can only be used for administering the UI program. Other limitations cited by state UI agencies include the lack of requirement for UI agencies to refer exhaustees to support programs, confidentiality laws, and the knowledge and training needed for UI staff to provide referrals to specific programs. In addition, one state UI agency noted that automation has been beneficial for reducing costs, but the corresponding reduction in in-person contact reduced the ability of the UI agency to refer people to other programs. In many states, UI claims are filed remotely, primarily by telephone or the Internet.

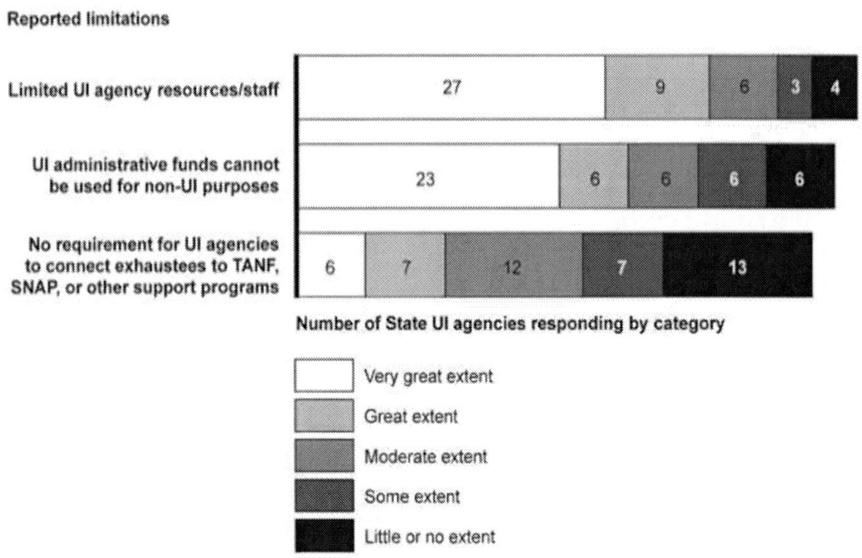

Source: GAO analysis of survey data.

Note: Totals do not add to 51 states because some states responded "don't know" or did not respond to this question.

Figure 10. Most Commonly Reported Limitations Associated with Connecting UI Exhaustees with TANF, SNAP, and Other Support Programs.

CONCLUSIONS

As the U.S. has faced the worst economic conditions since the 1930s, the UI program has played a critical role in helping millions of displaced workers through job losses. Despite the temporary benefit extensions, however, some individuals have exhausted UI benefits without a job, and a significant percentage have low incomes. As for the programs UI exhaustees and their households have turned to for additional assistance, few have received TANF as of 2009 in part because most do not match the target population of TANF. As currently financed and structured at the federal and state levels TANF does not appear to provide many of those we studied income support to help them weather the bad economic times. Some households have also turned to SNAP, whose financing and design may have helped it to expand with the poor economic conditions. Those eligible for Social Security retirement, disability, or survivors programs appear to have turned to those programs. While most state UI agencies already had efforts in place to help direct exhaustees to support programs, continued attention to outreach may help ensure that eligible people are connected to aid.

Sincerely yours,

Kay E. Brown
Director, Education, Workforce, and Income Security Issues

APPENDIX I: OBJECTIVES, SCOPE, AND METHODOLOGY

To address the objectives of this request, we used a variety of methods. Specifically, we

- analyzed pertinent data from two supplements to the Current Population Survey (CPS): the Displaced Worker Supplement and the Annual Social and Economic Supplement;
- conducted a web-based survey with Unemployment Insurance (UI) agencies in 50 states and the District of Columbia;
- conducted structured phone interviews with officials from 16 state Temporary Assistance for Needy Families (TANF) agencies;

- analyzed data on the UI program from the Department of Labor (Labor), on the TANF program from the Department of Health and Human Services (HHS), and on the Supplemental Nutrition Assistance Program (SNAP) from the U.S. Department of Agriculture (USDA); and
- conducted interviews with officials from Labor and HHS, as well as researchers, and reviewed applicable federal laws and regulations, studies, and policy documents.

Analysis of Displaced Worker Supplement Data

To identify the number of workers who received and exhausted UI, we used data from the biennial Displaced Worker Supplement to the Census Bureau's CPS. The CPS is the nation's source of official government statistics on employment and unemployment, and it is conducted on a monthly basis with about 60,000 households. Every 2 years with the January CPS, Census asks respondents 20 years or older whether they or someone in their household have experienced a job loss within the previous three years due to a plant or company closing or moving, insufficient work, or their position or shift being abolished. If a respondent answers yes, he or she is asked the questions in the Displaced Worker Supplement.[1] As such, for purposes of our review, a displaced worker is defined as a person who has experienced a job loss within the previous 3 years due to a plant or company closing or moving, insufficient work, or their position or shift being abolished. A person of any current employment status (employed, unemployed, or not in the labor force) may be classified as a displaced worker. For this review, we used data from the 2010 Displaced Worker Supplement (the most recent available), conducted in January 2010 with households in which someone lost a job from 2007 to 2009—the years of the recent recession.[2] For some of our analyses, we also compared the 2010 data to data from the 2008 Displaced Worker Supplement, conducted with households in which someone lost a job from 2005 to 2007, so that we could compare workers displaced during the recession to those displaced prior to the recession. Results of our review are as of January 2010 and January 2008, when the Displaced Worker Supplements were conducted.

We chose to use the Displaced Worker Supplement over other possible data sources, such as the Survey of Income and Program Participation, because the Displaced Worker Supplement contains questions to identify whether an individual who lost a job received and exhausted UI. For purposes of our review, we defined a UI exhaustee as a displaced worker with "yes" responses to the following two questions in the Displaced Workers Survey:

- "Did you receive unemployment insurance after that job (the job from which the worker was displaced) ended?" and
- "Did you exhaust your eligibility for unemployment benefits?"

We analyzed data from the Displaced Worker Supplement to estimate the percentage of displaced workers who received UI and the percentage who exhausted UI. We also used the data to examine the characteristics and labor force statuses of UI exhaustees specifically, in particular their ages, employment status at the time they were surveyed, and for those employed, their earnings at their new job compared to their previous job. Given the structure of the Displaced Worker Supplement, the survey captures the experiences of workers who lose jobs earlier in the 3-year period of the survey more fully than those who lost jobs later in the period, since more time would have elapsed between when they lost their job and when the survey was conducted. More specifically, the estimate of the number of displaced workers who exhausted UI does not include workers who may have exhausted UI at some point after January 2010.

In comparing UI receipt among higher-wage and lower-wage workers in the 2005-2007 and 2007-2009 time periods (using the 2008 and 2010 Displaced Worker Supplements, respectively), we conducted the analysis in two different ways and obtained virtually identical results. In the first approach, for each of the time periods, we compared displaced workers in the bottom 30 percent in average weekly wages with displaced workers in the top 70 percent, for the respondents with wage data available. Conducting the analysis in this way, displaced workers in the bottom 30 percent had average wages of $380 per week or less in the 2005-2007 time frame and average wages of $418 per week or less in the 2007-2009 time frame. In our second approach, we used the same average weekly wage as the cut-off point for defining the lower-wage worker group in the two time frames, adjusting for inflation. Specifically, lower-wage workers were still defined as those with average wages of $380 per week or less in 2005-2007. However, for 2007-2009, we used the $380 value to define the lower-wage group, but adjusted it for inflation. As such, displaced workers in the 2007-2009 time period were in the lower-wage group if they had average weekly wages of $400 or less. These two methods yielded results that were nearly identical. We presented the results of the first approach in figure 3.

Analysis of Displaced Worker Supplement Merged with the Annual Social and Economic Supplement

To examine the incomes of UI exhaustees and their receipt of benefits from government programs, we merged data from the Displaced Worker Supplement with data from the CPS' Annual Social and Economic Supplement (ASEC). Census conducts the ASEC annually to provide the usual monthly labor force data, as well as additional national data on work experience, income, and use of government benefits, among other topics. Due to the rotation structure of the CPS, approximately half of the households who were administered the Displaced Worker Supplement in January 2010 were also interviewed for the ASEC in March 2010.[3] Merging data from the two surveys allowed us to identify UI exhaustees (from the Displaced Worker Supplement) and examine their incomes (from the ASEC). Specifically, we used the merged data to examine UI exhaustees' private income sources, their family incomes relative to the federal poverty threshold, the presence of a child under the age of 18 in the household, and the benefits received from government programs. Data we report from the 2010 ASEC on the income status and receipt of benefits of UI exhaustees is for calendar year 2009. As such, our results may not necessarily reflect individuals' circumstances directly after exhausting their UI benefits, as we included all individuals who lost jobs from 2007 to 2009 and who then received and exhausted UI during that period and through January 2010, when the Displaced Worker Supplement was conducted.

Because the merged sample contains approximately half the number of observations as the full Displaced Worker Supplement sample, we inflated the population weights so that the weighted population counts from the merged sample would reflect the full displaced worker population. In addition, following the guidance of staff at the Bureau of Labor Statistics and the Census Bureau, we constructed raking factors to rebalance the merged sample by the race and ethnicity of the householder, the presence of children in the household, and the gender of the displaced worker. [4]

We used data in the ASEC to examine the incomes of UI exhaustees' households from both private and government sources. For each person in the sample 15 years old and over, the ASEC asks questions on the amount of money income received in the preceding calendar year from each of the following sources: earnings; unemployment compensation; workers' compensation; Social Security; Supplemental Security Income; public assistance; veterans' payments; survivors benefits; disability benefits; pension or retirement income; interest; dividends; rents, royalties, and estates and trusts; educational assistance; alimony; child support; regular financial assistance from outside of the household; and other periodic income. The income statistics in the ASEC refer to receipt of income during the preceding calendar year, in contrast to the demographic characteristics, such as age, labor force status, and family or household composition, which are as of the survey date. The income of the family/household does not include amounts received by people who were members during all or part of the income year if these people no longer resided in the family/household at the time of interview. However, the ASEC collects income data for people who are current residents but did not reside in the household during the income year.

Data on consumer income collected in the ASEC by the Census Bureau cover money income received (exclusive of certain money receipts such as capital gains) before payments for personal income taxes, Social Security, union dues, Medicare deductions, etc. Therefore, money income does not reflect the fact that some households receive part of their income in the form of noncash benefits, such as food stamps, health benefits, rent-free housing, and goods produced and consumed on the farm. In addition, money income does not reflect the fact that noncash benefits are also received by some nonfarm residents which often take the form of the use of business transportation and facilities, full or partial payments by business for retirement programs, medical and educational expenses, etc. Moreover, readers should be aware that for many different reasons there is a tendency in household surveys for respondents to underreport their income. Based on an analysis of independently derived income estimates, the Census Bureau determined that respondents report income earned from wages or salaries much better than other sources of income and that the reported wage and salary income is nearly equal to independent estimates of aggregate income.

We determined exhaustees' income-to-poverty ratios using Census computations. The Census classifies the income-to-poverty ratio of each family and unrelated individual using a poverty index adopted by the Federal Interagency Committee. The index provides a range of income cutoffs or "poverty thresholds" adjusted to take into account family size, number of children, and age of the family householder or unrelated individual. If a family's total money income is less than the applicable threshold, then that family and every individual in it are considered in poverty. The official poverty thresholds are updated annually for inflation using the Consumer Price Index. The official poverty definition uses money income before taxes and excludes capital gains and noncash benefits (such as SNAP benefits and housing assistance). The thresholds do not vary geographically.

We calculated standard errors for our estimates using the Census generalized variance functions, as published in the CPS January 2010 Displaced Worker, Employee Tenure, and Occupational Mobility Technical Documentation. However, we adjusted these standard error calculations to take account of the larger sampling interval of the merged sample, following guidance from staff at the Bureau of Labor Statistics and the Census Bureau.

We assessed the reliability of the CPS generally and of data elements that were critical to our analyses and determined that, despite the limitations outlined below, they were sufficiently reliable for our analyses. Specifically, we:

- reviewed documentation on the general design and methods of the CPS Displaced Worker Supplement and the CPS ASEC, and on the specific elements of the CPS data that were used in our analysis;
- interviewed Census Bureau and Bureau of Labor Statistics officials knowledgeable about the CPS data and consulted with these officials periodically throughout the course of our study; and
- completed our own electronic data testing to assess the accuracy and completeness of the data used in our analyses. To the extent possible, we compared our estimates against published reports using the CPS.

As a result of these efforts, we identified the following limitations with the data:

- The Census Bureau determined that respondents report income earned from wages or salaries much better than other sources of income. Therefore, estimates of receipt of government assistance may be underestimated.
- Due to the small sample sizes in our merged sample, confidence intervals around some of our estimates are wide. For these results, we report the upper bound of the 95 percent confidence interval.

Survey of State UI Agencies

To determine the extent to which UI agencies refer exhaustees to other programs, we conducted a web-based survey of state UI administrators in all 50 states and the District of Columbia. The survey was conducted from August to November 2011, with administrators from every state and the District of Columbia responding. The survey included questions about providing information to UI exhaustees about other support programs, coordinating or working with one-stops and/or workforce agencies, data on UI exhaustees, and changes states are making that may affect UI coverage.

Because this was not a sample survey, there are no sampling errors. However, the practical difficulties of conducting any survey may introduce nonsampling errors, such as variations in how respondents interpret questions and their willingness to offer accurate responses. We took steps to minimize nonsampling errors, including pretesting draft instruments and using a Web-based administration system. Specifically, during survey development, we pretested draft instruments with UI administrators from three states (Alabama, Arizona, and Pennsylvania) and a representative from the National Association of State Workforce Agencies in July 2011. We selected the pretest states to provide variation in selected state UI program characteristics and geographic location. In the pretests, we were generally interested in the clarity, precision, and objectivity of the questions, as well as the flow and layout of the survey. For example, we wanted to ensure definitions used in the surveys were clear and known to the respondents, categories provided in closed-ended questions were complete and exclusive, and the ordering of survey sections and the questions within each section was appropriate. We revised the final survey based on pretest results.

Another step we took to minimize nonsampling errors was using a web-based survey. Allowing respondents to enter their responses directly into an electronic instrument created a record for each respondent in a data file and eliminated the need for and the errors associated with a manual data entry process.

To further minimize errors, programs used to analyze the survey data and make estimations were independently verified to ensure the accuracy of this work.

While we did not fully validate specific information that states reported through our survey, we took several steps to ensure that the information was sufficiently reliable for the purposes of this chapter. For example, we reviewed the responses and identified those that required further clarification and, subsequently, conducted follow-up research to ensure the information they provided was reasonable and reliable. In our review of the data, we also identified and logically fixed skip pattern errors for questions that respondents should have skipped but did not. On the basis of these checks, we believe our survey data are sufficiently reliable for purposes of our work.

Interviews with State TANF Officials

To examine the role TANF played for individuals who lost jobs during the recession and its aftermath, we conducted semi-structured telephone interviews with TANF officials in 16 states. We pretested our questions with California and Pennsylvania. In our interviews we asked questions about the types of people seeking TANF, the types of services being provided, whether the state received TANF Emergency Contingency or TANF Contingency funds, challenges they faced in providing assistance to those in need, and their knowledge of whether a relationship exists between their agency and the state's UI program. The 16 states we selected to interview were chosen to represent a range of unemployment rates and TANF cash assistance caseloads and to achieve geographic diversity. The 16 states included in our analysis were: Alabama, Arkansas, California, Colorado, Florida, Illinois, Michigan, Minnesota, Montana, New York, North Carolina, Ohio, Pennsylvania, Rhode Island, Texas, and Washington state. Collectively these states represent more than half the families receiving ongoing TANF cash assistance nationally.

Analysis of Labor, HHS, and USDA Data

We analyzed relevant data from Labor to supplement our analysis of CPS data. Specifically, we analyzed Labor's data on UI claims to determine the number of people claiming UI benefits since 2007. We assessed the reliability of the data by interviewing Labor officials knowledgeable about the data, conducting electronic testing, and reviewing relevant documents. We determined that the data were sufficiently reliable for our purposes.

We also analyzed data on TANF and SNAP from HHS and USDA, respectively, for our background sections and text boxes.

Interviews with Agencies, Researchers, and Others

We interviewed officials from HHS and Labor about their UI and TANF programs and reviewed relevant federal laws and regulations, as well as guidance and other agency documentation. Additionally, we interviewed researchers and professionals from a variety of national organizations, including workforce and unemployment organizations, and reviewed available literature from these groups. These included the American Public Human

Services Association, National Employment Law Project, National Association of State Workforce Agencies, and the Urban Institute, among others.

End Notes

[1] The Bureau of Labor Statistics defines displaced workers as persons 20 years of age or older who lost or left jobs because their plant or company closed or moved, there was insufficient work for them to do, or their position or shift was abolished. Displaced workers are a distinct population from unemployed workers, since they may be employed, unemployed, or no longer in the labor force at a given point in time. The Bureau of Labor Statistics defines unemployed workers as persons who do not have a job, have actively looked for a job in the past 4 weeks, and are currently available for work. Unemployed workers includes several groups of workers who would not be considered displaced workers, including new entrants to the labor force and those who left jobs for reasons other than displacement, such as voluntary quits or firings.

[2] The $156 billion is as of fiscal year 2010.

[3] The term exhaustee is used by the UI program. For the purposes of this chapter, we define a UI exhaustee as a displaced worker with "yes" responses to the following two questions in the Displaced Worker Supplement: (1) "Did you receive unemployment insurance after that job (the job from which the worker was displaced) ended?," and (2) "Did you exhaust your eligibility for unemployment benefits?" As used in this chapter, the term includes all exhaustees, regardless of whether they were employed, unemployed, or not in the labor force at the time of the survey.

[4] Specifically, we merged data of individuals who were surveyed by the Census Bureau both in January 2010 for the Displaced Worker Supplement and in March 2010 for the Annual Social and Economic Supplement. Approximately 50 percent of the respondents in the Displaced Worker Supplement were also surveyed for the Annual Social and Economic Supplement.

[5] We include the District of Columbia in our discussion of states.

[6] The proportion of workers' wages replaced by UI benefits is known as the replacement rate. According to Labor's data, the average replacement rates in 2010 ranged from 33 percent to 57 percent among the states.

[7] Congressional Research Service, Unemployment Insurance: Available Benefits and Legislative Activity (Washington, D.C.: Dec 21, 2010).

[8] Department of Labor, Significant Provisions of State Unemployment Insurance Laws, Effective July 2011.

[9] Pub. L. No. 111-5, § 2005(a), 123 Stat. 115, 444. 10Pub. L. No. 112-78, § 201(a)(2), 125 Stat. 1280, 1282.

[11] Pub. L. No. 110-449, § 2, 122 Stat. 5014. Congress created the current temporary Emergency Unemployment Compensation program in the Supplemental Appropriations Act, 2008. Pub. L. No. 110-252, Title IV, 122 Stat. 2323, 2353. Congress extended this program several times, most recently in the Temporary Payroll Tax Cut Continuation Act of 2011 (Pub. L. No. 112-78, § 201(a)(1), 125 Stat. 1280, 1282).

[12] Pub. L. No. 104-193, § 103, 110 Stat. 2105, 2112.

[13] To be counted as engaging in work activities for a month, most families receiving TANF cash assistance are required to participate in work activities for an average of 30 hours per week in that month. There are 12 work activities that may count toward meeting the specified work participation rate: unsubsidized employment, subsidized private sector employment, subsidized public sector employment, work experience (if sufficient private sector employment is not available), on-the-job training, job search and job readiness assistance, community service programs, vocational education training, job skills training directly related to employment, education directly related to employment (if the recipient has not received a high school diploma or certificate of high school equivalence), satisfactory secondary school attendance or in a course of study leading to a certificate of general equivalence, and providing child care services to others in community service.

[14] Generally speaking, states are required to have 50 percent of all families receiving ongoing cash assistance participate in work activities and 90 percent of two-parent families. However, states can reduce the rates they are required to meet by reducing their cash assistance caseloads or by using more state funds than required to provide assistance to some families. Some families are excluded from these work requirements, such as those in which children alone receive the cash assistance benefits. States may also disregard certain other families from the work participation rate, such as families in which a single custodial parent is caring for a child under age one (for not more than 12 months over a person's lifetime). For further information on work participation rates, see GAO, Temporary Assistance for Needy Families, Implications of Recent Legislative and Economic Changes for State Programs and Work Participation Rates, GAO-10-525 (Washington, D.C.: May 28, 2010).

[15] Pub. L. No. 111-5, § 2101, 123 Stat. 115, 446. For information on subsidized employment programs supported by TANF Recovery Act funds, see Mary Farrell, Sam Elkin, Joseph Broadus, and Dan Bloom, Subsidized Employment Opportunities for Low-Income Families: A Review of State Employment Programs Created Through the TANF Emergency Fund, OPRE Report 2011-38, Washington, DC: Office of Planning, Research and Evaluation, Administration for Children and Families, U.S. Department of Health and Human Services, 2011.

[16] Specifically, based on the Bureau of Labor Statistics' definition, these displaced workers are persons 20 years of age and older who lost or left jobs within the 3 years prior to the survey because their plant or company closed or moved, there was insufficient work for them to do, or their position or shift was abolished.

[17] See GAO, Unemployment Insurance: Low-Wage and Part-Time Workers Continue to Experience Low Rates of Receipt, GAO-07-1147 (Washington, D.C.: Sept. 7, 2007) and Unemployment Insurance: Role as Safety Net for Low-Wage Workers Is Limited, GAO-01-181 (Washington, D.C.: Dec. 29, 2000), which examined selected years in the 1990s and 2003. Another GAO study examining a cohort of individuals born between 1957 and 1964 and their labor market experiences from 1979 to 2002 also found that unemployed workers with higher earnings were more likely to receive UI benefits. See GAO, Unemployment Insurance: Factors Associated with Benefit Receipt, GAO-06-341 (Washington, D.C.: Mar. 7, 2006).

[18] In our prior work, we noted that individuals generally must have become unemployed involuntarily or for "good cause" to be eligible for UI. We and others found variation among states in the circumstances which constitute "good cause." For example, some states had policies allowing individuals to be eligible for UI if they left a job to care for a sick child or due to domestic violence, while others did not. See GAO-01-181 and GAO-07-

1174; Wayne Vroman, Low Benefit Recipiency in State Unemployment Insurance Programs (June 2001); and Lewin Group, Unemployment Insurance Non-Monetary Policies and Practices: How Do They Affect Program Participation? A Study of 8 States (Jan. 31, 2003).

[19] Pub. L. No. 111-5, § 2003, 123 Stat. 115, 439.

[20] We previously reported that the severity and length of the recent recession, and the slow pace of recovery, have placed a heavy demand on state UI trust funds, and many states have needed loans from the federal government to continue to pay benefits. See GAO, Unemployment Insurance Trust Funds: Long-standing State Financing Policies Have Increased Risk of Insolvency, GAO-10-440 (Washington, D.C.: Apr. 14, 2010).

[21] For purposes of this chapter, we define a UI exhaustee as a displaced worker with a "yes" response to the following two questions in the Displaced Worker Supplement: (1) "Did you receive unemployment insurance after that job (the job from which the worker was displaced) ended?" and (2) "Did you exhaust your eligibility for unemployment benefits?"

[22] Given the structure of the Displaced Worker Supplement, workers who lose jobs earlier in the 3-year period of the survey would be more likely to have exhausted UI benefits by the time of the survey, since more time would have elapsed between when they lost their job and when the survey was conducted. Among those surveyed in the 2010 Displaced Worker Supplement, 46 percent of those who lost jobs in 2007 exhausted their UI benefits by January 2010, 32 percent of those who lost jobs in 2008 exhausted their UI benefits, and 18 percent of those who lost jobs in 2009 exhausted their UI benefits. For the 2008 Displaced Worker Supplement, UI exhaustion rates were 50 percent for those who lost jobs in 2005 and received UI, 55 percent for 2006, and 33 percent for 2007.

[23] The estimates from Labor are of all UI claimants who exhausted UI, and therefore may not be comparable to the estimate of the number of UI exhaustees from the Displaced Worker Supplement, which are of displaced workers who received and exhausted UI.

[24] The high percentage of re-employed exhaustees experiencing earnings reduction likely reflects the fact that UI exhaustees were unemployed for long durations. Research has found that longer durations of unemployment are associated with reduced earnings levels at the workers' new jobs. There are many possible reasons for this, such as diminished job prospects as workers lose job skills or networks during the period of unemployment, a possible stigma associated with long-term unemployment, and greater willingness to take jobs at reduced wages the longer a worker searches for a job. See Congressional Budget Office, Long-Term Unemployment (Washington, D.C.: October 2007); and John T. Addison and Pedro Portugal, "Job Displacement, Relative Wage Changes, and Duration of Unemployment," Journal of Labor Economics, 7:3 (July 1989).

[25] The data we present on poverty rates and income-to-poverty ratios are based on Census computations of income-to-poverty ratios in the Annual Social and Economic Supplement. The federal poverty threshold varies by family size. For example, in 2009, a family of one person under the age of 65 with total income below $11,161 was considered to be in poverty, while a family of four (two adults and two children under age 18) with total income below $21,756 was in poverty. With regard to the percentage of UI exhaustees in poverty, annual income data may not capture families who were in poverty for only part of the year.

[26] Nationally, 47 percent of working-age civilian adults (age 18-64) had a child age 18 or under in their household.

[27] Urban Institute, Welfare Rules Databook: State TANF Policies as of July 2009 (August 2010). Not all households with income below the federal poverty threshold and minor children are

eligible for TANF. In some states, families with children must have income below the federal poverty level to be initially eligible for ongoing TANF cash assistance, and in other states, their income must be well below the federal poverty level. There are other factors considered in determining a families' eligibility for TANF benefits, which vary by state, such as the family's assets, immigration status, and whether a family previously received TANF cash assistance and reached the time limit on benefits. Different eligibility criteria may apply to one-time benefits. In addition, TANF eligibility is established on a monthly basis, while the CPS provides data on annual income. As such, families who were in poverty for part of 2009 might have been eligible for TANF in some months of 2009, even though their annual income was above the federal poverty threshold in 2009.

[28] These data are derived from a question in the 2010 Annual Social and Economic Supplement to the CPS, which asked respondents the following: "At any time during 2009, even for one month, did (you/anyone in the household) receive any cash assistance from a state or county welfare program such as (name of the program in respondent's state). Include cash payments from: welfare or welfare-to-work programs, state program name and/or acronyms, Temporary Assistance for Needy Families (TANF), Aid to Families with Dependent Children (AFDC), General Assistance/Emergency Assistance program, Diversion Payments, Refugee Cash and Medical Assistance program, General Assistance from Bureau of Indian Affairs, or Tribal Administered General Assistance." Many of these welfare programs, including Diversion Payments, welfare or welfare-to-work programs, and state programs, are within the TANF program. AFDC is the name of the former welfare program, which was replaced by TANF in 1996. The CPS data provide information on households' receipt of financial assistance from TANF but do not provide information on receipt of non-cash assistance or services from TANF.

[29] The Supplemental Security Income program provides benefits to people with low incomes who are blind, disabled, or are age 65 and older.

[30] The earliest age at which an individual can begin receiving Social Security retirement benefits is age 62, though benefits are reduced for those who draw them prior to the full retirement age. The full retirement age ranges from 65 to 67, depending upon a person's year of birth.

[31] This is meant to illustrate receipt of TANF and other government benefits among relatively low-income families of UI exhaustees with minor children. Not all families with children and incomes below 200 percent of the federal poverty threshold are eligible for TANF benefits. While families generally must have income below the federal poverty threshold to be initially eligible for ongoing TANF cash assistance, in many states, once a family has been receiving TANF benefits, income earned from employment may be disregarded for some time to compensate for work-related expenses or to serve as an incentive to work. This means that a family with income greater than the level for initial eligibility may continue to receive TANF. Urban Institute, Welfare Rules Databook. See footnote 27 for further information on TANF eligibility criteria.

[32] Urban Institute, Welfare Rules Databook: State TANF Policies as of July 2009. In 2009, most states had asset limits ranging from $1,000 to $3,000, with the value of a home and the value of at least one vehicle exempted.

[33] TANF cash assistance benefit levels vary by state. In 2009, maximum monthly benefits across the states ranged from $170 to $923 for a family of three, with a median benefit of $429. Congressional Research Service, The Temporary Assistance for Needy Families (TANF) Block Grant: Responses to Frequently Asked Questions (Washington, D.C.: Dec. 27, 2011).

[34] Federal law limits the number of weekly hours that TANF families can participate in three activities and have them count toward their work requirements: education directly related to

employment (for recipients who have not received a high school diploma or a high school equivalency), job skills training directly related to employment, and satisfactory attendance at secondary school or in a course of study leading to a certificate of general equivalency. There are also limits on the amount of time states can count each family's participation in two other work activities—job search and job readiness assistance, and vocational education. The time limit on job search and job readiness assistance is generally 6 weeks, but states can extend this limit to 12 weeks during times of economic distress. The time limit on vocational education is 12 months over a person's lifetime.

[35] For more information on receipt of TANF among eligible families, see GAO, Temporary Assistance for Needy Families: Fewer Eligible Families Have Received Cash Assistance Since the 1990s, and the Recession's Impact on Caseloads Varies by State, GAO-10-164 (Washington, D.C.: Feb. 23, 2010).

[36] For the purposes of our survey of the 51 state UI agencies, the UI agencies were instructed that support programs included TANF, SNAP, disability benefits (e.g., Supplemental Security Income, and Social Security Disability Insurance), state and county income support programs, food banks, and other assistance programs. We generally asked about groups of programs and not about each program individually.

[37] 42 U.S.C. § 502(a).

End Notes for Appendix I

[1] Respondents who said they or a household member were no longer working due to other reasons, such as a seasonal job being completed or failure of a self-operated business, are not classified as displaced workers and are not asked the questions in the Displaced Worker Supplement.

[2] The National Bureau of Economic Research Business Cycle Dating Committee announced the official beginning of the recession as December 2007 and the official end as June 2009.

[3] Households interviewed for the CPS are administered the survey for 4 consecutive months, then are not interviewed for 8 months, and then are interviewed for an additional 4 months. Each month, one-eighth of households are being surveyed for the first time, one-eighth for the second time, one-eighth for the third time, etc. With this rotation, approximately half of the households interviewed in January 2010 were also interviewed in March 2010, and therefore were administered both the Displaced Worker Supplement if they were eligible and the ASEC.

[4] Specifically, the ASEC oversamples a group referred to as the "Children's Health Insurance Program (CHIP) expansion sample." This is defined as any households where the householder is minority (either non-White or Hispanic), and/or any household that contains at least one child (18 years or under). Because the merged sample included members of the "CHIP expansion sample," we raked the weights so observations in the "CHIP expansion sample" are not over-represented in the data. A raking factor is a number multiplied by the population weight to rebalance the sample. We also raked the weights by gender of the displaced worker and race/ethnicity of the householder, to control for any sample attrition along these variables. Following the guidance of the Census Bureau, we restricted our raking factors to cells with a minimum of 30 observations, and to factors that met Census Bureau guidelines for size.

In: High Unemployment: Select Analyses
Editors: L. Sandidge and V. Irby
ISBN: 978-1-62257-994-5

Chapter 3

ECONOMIC GROWTH AND THE UNEMPLOYMENT RATE*

Linda Levine

SUMMARY

A persistently high unemployment rate is of concern to Congress for a variety of reasons, including its negative consequences for the economic well-being of individuals and its impact on the federal budget (i.e., deficit growth due to lower revenue and higher expenditures). The unemployment rate was 9.5% when the economy emerged from the 11th postwar recession in June 2009. It climbed further to peak at 10.1% in October 2009. The rate then slowly declined before stalling at about 9.0% for most of 2011. Although the unemployment rate has resumed its decline, at slightly above 8.0% in early 2012, it remains at an historically high level.

The slow rebound of the labor market has prompted calls for new measures to stimulate economic growth to avoid a so-called double-dip recession, such as occurred during the early 1980s. The economy contracted in July 1981, 12 months into the recovery from the January-July 1980 recession. The unemployment rate had not fallen to its pre-recession level before the 1981-1982 recession began. Some observers have from time to time expressed concern that another shock (e.g., the

* This is an edited, reformatted and augmented version of a Congressional Research Service publication, CRS Report for Congress R42063, prepared for Members and Committees of Congress, dated April 18, 2012.

slowdown of European economies) might push the nation back into recession.

After most postwar recessions, it took at least eight months for the unemployment rate to fall by one full percentage point. The slowest decline occurred following the 2001 recession's end, when the unemployment rate was a comparatively low 5.5%. About 31/2 years elapsed before the rate fell just one-half of one percentage point. In contrast, the recovery from the severe 1981-1982 recession began with the highest unemployment rate of the postwar period (10.8%). In that instance, it took only eight months for the rate to fall over one percentage point. Some hoped the unemployment rate would fall as quickly after the Great Recession, but the speed of improvement has been more typical of the so-called jobless recovery from the 2001 recession.

What appears to matter for a reduction in the unemployment rate is the size of the output gap, that is, the rate of actual economic growth compared with the rate of potential output growth. Potential output is a measure of the economy's capacity to produce goods and services when resources (e.g., labor) are fully utilized. The growth rate of potential output is a function of the growth rates of potential productivity and the labor supply when the economy is at full employment. If potential output growth is about 2.5% annually at full employment, then the growth rate in real gross domestic product (GDP) would have to be greater to yield a falling unemployment rate. How much greater will determine the speed of improvement in the unemployment rate, according to a rule of thumb known as Okun's law.

Some observers recently have suggested that the decline in the unemployment rate from 9.0% in September 2011 to 8.5% in December 2011 defied Okun's law because real GDP growth appears to have been too low to have produced such a large fall in unemployment. With the Congressional Budget Office (CBO) projecting that real GDP growth will stay below potential output growth for years to come, the unemployment rate may remain about where it is today (above 8.0%) through 2014, before falling to less than 6.0% by 2017.

INTRODUCTION

Despite the resumption of economic (output) growth in June 2009, the unemployment rate remains at an historically high level almost three years into the recovery from the 11th recession of the postwar period. The unemployment rate has settled at a little over 8.0% during the first few months of 2012.

The slow rebound of the labor market has renewed calls for measures to stimulate the economy beyond those Congress has previously enacted.[1] It has, from time to time, prompted speculation about a so-called double-dip recession[2] that might result from another shock to the U.S. economy (e.g., the slowdown of European economies).

From a public policy perspective, the main driver of the unemployment rate is the pace of economic growth. This chapter first examines the long-run relationship between the two economic variables and then narrows its focus to the periods of recovery from the postwar recessions.

THE RELATIONSHIP BETWEEN GROWTH AND UNEMPLOYMENT

In the short run, the relationship between economic growth and the unemployment rate may be a loose one. It is not unusual for the unemployment rate to show sustained decline some time after other broad measures of economic activity have turned positive. Hence, it is commonly referred to as a lagging economic indicator. One reason that unemployment may not fall appreciably when economic growth first picks up after a recession's end is that some firms may have underutilized employees on their payrolls because laying off workers when product demand declines and rehiring them when product demand improves has costs. (This is referred to as labor hoarding.) As a result, employers may initially be able to increase output to meet rising demand at the outset of a recovery without hiring additional workers by raising the productivity of their current employees. This temporarily boosts labor productivity growth above its trend (long-run) rate.

Once the labor on hand is fully utilized, however, output can grow no faster than the rate of growth of labor productivity until firms begin adding workers. As an economic expansion progresses, output growth will be determined by the combined rates of growth in the labor supply and labor productivity. As long as growth in real gross domestic product (GDP) exceeds growth in labor productivity, employment will rise. If employment growth is more rapid than labor force growth, the unemployment rate will fall.

Over an extended period of time, there is an inverse (negative) relationship between changes in the rates of real GDP growth and unemployment. This long-run relationship between the two economic variables was most famously pointed out in the early 1960s by economist Arthur Okun. "Okun's law" has been included in a list of "core ideas" that are widely accepted in the economics profession.[3] Okun's law, which economists have expanded upon since it was first articulated, states that real GDP growth about equal to the rate of potential output growth usually is required to maintain a stable unemployment rate.[4]

Thus, the key to the long-run relationship between changes in the rates of GDP growth and unemployment is the rate of growth in potential output. Potential output is an unobservable measure of the capacity of the economy to produce goods and services when available resources, such as labor and capital, are fully utilized. The rate of growth of potential output is a function of the rate of growth in potential productivity and the labor supply when the economy is at full employment.[5] When the unemployment rate is high, as it is now, then actual GDP falls short of potential GDP. This is referred to as the output gap.

In the absence of productivity growth, as long as each new addition to the labor force is employed, growth in output will equal growth in the labor supply. If the rate of GDP growth falls below the rate of labor force growth, there will not be enough new jobs created to accommodate all new job seekers. As a result, the proportion of the labor force that is employed will fall. Put differently, the unemployment rate will rise. If the rate of output growth exceeds the rate of labor force growth, some of the new jobs created by employers to satisfy the rising demand for their goods and services will be filled by drawing from the pool of unemployed workers. In other words, the unemployment rate will fall.[6]

If GDP growth equals labor force growth in the presence of productivity growth, more people will be entering the labor force than are needed to produce a given amount of goods and services. The share of the labor force that is employed will fall. Expressed differently, the unemployment rate will rise. Only as long as GDP growth exceeds the combined growth rates of the labor force and productivity (potential output) will the unemployment rate fall in the long run.

Knowing what that rate of GDP growth is might be useful to policymakers interested in undertaking stimulus policies to bring down the unemployment rate. But as just stated, the rate of output growth necessary to lower the unemployment rate requires knowledge of the rates of labor force and productivity growth. Both have changed over time.

Between 1950 and 2000, the civilian labor force grew at an average annual rate of 1.6%.[7] The growth rate has slowed since then and is expected to continue doing so partly as a result of the aging of the baby-boom generation. Between 2000 and 2010, the annual rate of labor force growth fell to 0.8%. It is projected to fall further, to 0.7% per year on average, between 2010 and 2020.[8]

Predicting productivity growth is more difficult than predicting labor force growth. Economists had, until recently, identified three time periods that correspond with three different trend rates of growth in productivity.[9] Between 1947 and 1973, output per hour of labor in the private nonfarm business sector grew at an annual rate of 2.8%. Between 1973 and 1995, productivity slowed to an annual average rate of 1.4%. Between 1995 and 2005, it accelerated to 2.9% per year. Since then (2005-2011), the rate of productivity growth has slowed to 1.6% annually.[10]

If recent trends in labor force and productivity growth continue, real GDP growth above about 2.5% will be needed to push down the unemployment rate from its currently elevated level. "More specifically, according to currently accepted versions of Okun's law, to achieve a 1 percentage point decline in the unemployment rate in the course of a year, real GDP must grow approximately 2 percentage points faster than the rate of growth of potential GDP over that period."[11]

THE UNEMPLOYMENT RATE DURING POSTWAR RECOVERIES

As previously discussed, it is not unusual for some time to elapse between the start of an economic recovery and the start of a declining unemployment rate. Suppose that two successive monthly declines are taken as the beginning of a meaningful downward trend in the unemployment rate. *Table 1* shows how long it has taken following the end of each of the 11 economic contractions for that trend to begin.

At one extreme, it was well over a year following the start of the economy's rebound from the 1990-1991 and 2001 recessions before the unemployment rate began to steadily decline. This contributed to the two periods being labeled jobless recoveries. At the other extreme, the unemployment rate began trending downward at five or fewer months after the end of five earlier recessions.

The current recovery lies within but closer to the high-end of this range. As the unemployment rate experienced two successive monthly declines 12 months after the start of the recovery from the 2007-2009 recession, it too was dubbed a jobless recovery.

Table 1. Months Between the Start of a Recovery and Two Successive Declines in the Unemployment Rate

Date of Start of Recovery	Months After Recovery's Start and Two Successive Declines in Unemployment Rate
October 1949	4
May 1954	6
April 1958	5
February 1961	9
November 1970	11
March 1975	4
July 1980	2
November 1982	5
March 1991	17
November 2001	21
June 2009	12

Source: Calculated by CRS based on business cycle troughs from the National Bureau of Economic Research and unemployment rates from the U.S. Bureau of Labor Statistics.

Not only has the length of time for the unemployment rate to begin falling varied by recovery, but its pace of decline also has varied. After eight of the eleven postwar recessions, it took at least eight months for the unemployment rate to fall by one full percentage point.[12] The slowest decline occurred after the recession that ended in November 2001 when the unemployment rate stood at 5.5%, the lowest unemployment rate recorded at the start of an expansion. About 31/2 years elapsed before the unemployment rate fell one-half of a percentage point. In contrast, the expansion that followed the July 1981-November 1982 downturn began with the highest unemployment rate of the postwar period (10.8%). In that case, it took only eight months for the unemployment rate to fall more than one percentage point (to a still high 9.4%).

Some have from time to time suggested that the nation may be heading toward another recession so close in time to the end of the 2007-2009 recession that they are referred to collectively as a double-dip recession. This rare situation last occurred following the 1980 recession: the unemployment at almost three years after its June 1980 trough was above 10.0%, more than 2 percentage points higher than at the recession's end; this occurred because the expansion only lasted a year before another recession began in July 1981. In contrast, the unemployment rate of slightly above 8.0% almost three years into the recovery from the 2007-2009 recession remains below its level of 9.5% at the recession's trough in June 2009. This suggests that a double-dip recession is not in the offing absent a shock to the U.S. economy from the slowdown in the economies of Europe, for example.

A debate recently broke out over the applicability of Okun's law to changes in economic growth and the unemployment rate in 2011.[13] Following a period of growth rates early in the recovery high enough (above 3.5%) to have produced a downward trend in the unemployment rate, the unemployment rate stalled at about 9.0% in the first three quarters of 2011. This resulted from slow annual growth in real GDP of 0.4% in the first quarter, 1.3% in the second quarter, and 1.8% in the third quarter of 2011.[14] Output growth accelerated at an annual rate of 3.0% in the fourth quarter of 2011, and the unemployment rate resumed its downward trend—dropping 0.5 percentage points to 8.5% in December 2011.

But as noted by the chairman of the Federal Reserve Board at a March 2012 conference of economists,

> the decline in the unemployment rate over the course of 2011 was greater than would seem consistent with GDP growth over that period. Indeed, with last year's real GDP growth below 2 percent, less than what most economists would estimate to be the U.S. economy's potential rate of growth, one might have expected little change in the unemployment rate last year or even a slight increase.[15]

Bernanke suggests that this temporary disconnect may be compensating for an earlier deviation from Okun's law. In 2009, workers were laid off and the unemployment rate rose beyond the level commensurate with the contraction in economic growth.

Neither Bernanke nor Burgen, Meyer, and Tasci at the Cleveland Federal Reserve Bank think that much of the Okun's law puzzle will be solved after the Bureau of Economic Analysis makes its periodic revisions of the quarterly GDP estimates for 2011.[16] When McCarthy, Potter, and Ng at the New York Federal Reserve Bank examined a longer recovery period after the trough of the last three recessions,[17] they estimated that Okun's law underpredicted the actual decline in the unemployment rate. The analysis led them to conclude that Okun's rule of thumb "has not been a reliable indicator of unemployment declines over long periods of recent expansions"— particularly during the jobless recoveries that followed the 1990-1991 and 2001 recessions.[18] Others similarly have demonstrated periods of instability in the long-run relationship between economic growth and unemployment. Some of the variation appears to be due to the state of the business cycle, both in terms of recessions compared with recoveries and the longer-than-average length of expansions following recent recessions.[19]

THE OUTLOOK FOR THE UNEMPLOYMENT RATE IN THE NEXT FEW YEARS

According to estimates by economist Robert J. Gordon, potential output has grown at an average annual rate of 3.4% since 1875.[20] Gordon doubts, however, that growth in potential GDP will be that rapid over the next 20 years as gains from information technology investments have been diminishing. His assumption of slower productivity growth along with the previously discussed expected declines in labor force growth led him to project a 2.4% rate of growth in potential output over the next 20 years. If that view is correct, then real economic growth in excess of 2.4% would be likely to yield a declining rate of unemployment.

Economists Susanto Basu and John G. Fernald also examined the current outlook for growth in potential output.[21] They point out that household net worth declined significantly during the 2007-2009 recession. That drop in wealth, they argue, will make it more difficult for workers to afford leisure time (e.g., retirement). Consequently, the supply of labor may be larger in the near term than it might otherwise have been. This would tend to temporarily raise growth in potential output. At the same time, Basu and Fernald expect that disruptions in financial markets will tend to constrain growth in potential output over the near term because of higher risks associated with investment spending. These offsetting factors mainly serve to emphasize how uncertain estimates of growth in potential output can be.

Weidner and Williams examined the relationship between real economic growth and the strength of past recoveries. The economists estimate that potential output growth was comparatively rapid during the initial expansions of the 1960s through 1980s (at 3.6%). In contrast, potential output was much more moderate (2.5%) during the first two years of recovery from the 1990-1991 and 2001 recessions. They estimate potential GDP growth at the outset of the recovery from the Great Recession was a more sluggish 2.1% due to the slow rate of labor force growth.[22] If they are correct, real economic growth greater than 2.1% would likely produce a falling unemployment rate.

The Congressional Budget Office (CBO) publishes projections of growth in potential output. In its latest economic outlook, CBO forecast that potential output of the overall economy will grow at an average annual rate of 2.3% between 2012 and 2022.[23] In contrast, CBO estimated a considerably higher average annual growth rate of potential GDP over the 1950-2010 period (3.3%). The lower projection of potential output growth going forward chiefly reflects CBO's projection of diminishing potential labor force growth.

According to CBO's most recent forecast for the 2012-2022 period, the annual average growth rate of real GDP will stay below potential output for several years to come. As a result, CBO projects that the unemployment rate will remain above 8.0%—about where it is today—through 2014, before declining to less than 6.0% by 2017.

End Notes

[1] For additional information, see CRS Report R41578, Unemployment: Issues in the 112th Congress, by Jane G. Gravelle, Thomas L. Hungerford, and Linda Levine.

[2] For additional information, see CRS Report R41444, Double-Dip Recession: Previous Experience and Current Prospect, by Craig K. Elwell.

[3] Alan Blinder, "Is There A Core of Practical Macroeconomics That We Should All Believe?," American Economic Review, vol. 87, no. 2, May 1997.

[4] Knotek updated Okun's analysis, which covered the 1948-1960 period, to 2007 and came to much the same conclusion. Specifically, real output growth of about 4.0% is consistent with a stable unemployment rate. This means that in the long run faster output growth usually coincided with a decreasing unemployment rate, whereas output growth below 4% usually coincided with an increasing unemployment rate. See Edward S. Knotek, "How Useful is Okun's Law?," Federal Reserve Bank of Kansas City, Economic Review, fourth quarter 2007. (Hereafter referred to as Knotek, How Useful is Okun's Law.)

[5] Full employment is said to be achieved when the unemployment rate is at a level consistent with a stable (non-accelerating) inflation rate.

[6] Once unemployment reaches relatively low levels, the increased demand for labor is more likely to be satisfied by rising wages than by higher levels of employment. There may be a risk of accelerating inflation as a result. The Congressional Budget Office estimated that the rate close to which that becomes a risk (which is referred to as the nonaccelerating inflation rate of unemployment or NAIRU) may be about 5%. (See Robert Arnold, Reestimating the Phillips Curve and the NAIRU, CBO, Working Paper 2008-06, August 2008.) At the current level of the unemployment rate, the risk of accelerating wages and inflation seems low. It also seems low at even higher estimates of NAIRU, which ranged from 6.2% to 8.2% for the first quarter of 2011 according to estimates by Weidner and Williams (Update of "How Big is the Output Gap?," Federal Reserve Bank of San Francisco, July 7, 2011).

[7] Mitra Toossi, "A Century of Change: the U.S. Labor Force, 1950-2050," Monthly Labor Review, May 2002.

[8] Mitra Toossi, "Labor Force Projections to 2020: A More Slowly Growing Workforce," January 2012.

[9] See for example Michael Chernousov, Susan E. Fleck, and John Glaser, "Productivity Trends in Business Cycles," Monthly Labor Review, June 2009; and J. Bradford DeLong, "Productivity Growth in the 2000s," National Bureau of Economic Research, Macroeconomics Annual, vol. 17 (2000).

[10] Calculated by CRS from BLS productivity data, available at http://www.bls.gov.

[11] Chairman Ben S. Bernanke at the National Association for Business Economics annual conference, Washington, DC, March 26, 2012, available at http://www.federalreserve.gov/ newsevents/speech/bernanke 20120326a.htm. (Hereafter referred to as Bernanke, NABE conference address.)

[12] They are the recoveries from the 1960-1961, 1969-1970, 1973-1975, 1980, 1981-1982, 1990-1991, 2001, and 2007- 2009 recessions.

[13] See for example Nin-Hai Tseng, "Jobless Numbers Defy Economic Theory," CNNMoney, March 15, 2012, available at http://finance. fortune.cnn.com/2012/03/16/okuns-law/.

[14] U.S. Bureau of Economic Analysis, National Income and Product Accounts data available at http://www.bea.gov.

[15] Bernanke, NABE conference address.

[16] Emily Burgen, Brent Meyer, and Murat Tasci, "An Elusive Relation between Unemployment and GDP Growth: Okun's Law," Cleveland Federal Reserve Economic Trends, April 5, 2012.

[17] Years two through five from the end of the 1981-1982, 1990-1991, and 2001 recessions.

[18] Jonathan McCarthy, Simon Potter, and Ging Cee Ng, "Okun's Law and Long Expansions," Federal Reserve Bank of New York, March 27, 2012, available at http://liberty street economics.newyorkfed.org/2012/03/okuns-law-and-longexpansions.html.

[19] Knotek, How Useful Is Okun's Law.

[20] Robert J. Gordon, "The Slowest Potential Output Growth in U.S. History: Measurement and Interpretation," presented at the Center for the Study of Innovation and Productivity at the Federal Reserve Bank of San Francisco, November 2008.

[21] Susanto Basu and John G. Fernald, What Do We Know and Not Know About Potential Output?, Federal Reserve Bank of San Francisco, Working Paper, March 2009.

[22] Justin Weidner and John C. Williams, "The Shape of Things to Come," Federal Reserve Bank of San Francisco, Economic Letter, May 17, 2010.

[23] Congressional Budget Office, The Budget and Economic Outlook: Fiscal Years 2012 to 2022, January 2012.

INDEX

D

E

I

J

L

M

N

O

P

R

S

Y